Luminous Leaders

Amanda M Renaud, Maria Rekrut, Sammie Lee Hill, Antoine Airoldi, Lisa Rickards, Mark Bentcover, May Baydoun & Dr. Michael Noble Emeghara

Legal Disclaimer

Luminous Leaders

ASIN NUMBER: B0DNCPLBXC EBOOK

ASIN: B0DNCPW5Q6 Paperback

Luminous Leaders

~ Dedication ~

This book is dedicated to all the leaders who have struggled, failed, and ever made mistakes. No matter how hard the journey of leadership become— keep going!

~ Acknowledgments ~

We would like to acknowledge Rev Dr. Marianne Padjan and Dr. Robert J Moore the former Founder of Magnetic Entrepreneur Inc & the current CEO Amanda M Renaud for her hard work & dedication to make this book come to life. This book giving leaders an opportunity to share their wisdom and knowledge.

Table of Contents

Contents

Luminous Leaders

Amanda M Renaud

.

Luminous Leaders

~ Amanda M Renaud ~

Amanda M Renaud is the CEO of formerly Magnetic Entrepreneur Inc, founded by Robert J Moore a New York Times Best selling Author. Amanda has rebranded to Magnetic Publishing. Magnetic has been featured in Forbes, USA today, Disrupt Magazine, Yahoo finance and many other places globally. Magnetic Entrepreneur holds a Guinness world record and has recently won a Global Recognition Award for 2023. Amanda aspires to carry out the legacy and accolades of Robert J Moore.

Magnetic Publishing focuses on providing quality book publishing services as well as provides its clients with coaching services. Magnetic Entrepreneur excels in creating Best Selling Authors, as an International Best Seller herself.

Amanda is a certified Transformational coach, Mentor for APLGO and holds an advanced diploma in Child and Youth Treatment. Amanda is a known Canadian Entrepreneur and Author who focuses on Health and Wellness as well as Leadership. Amanda released her first solo book this past October 2023 called Exceptional Minds a novel written to help Leaders and Entrepreneurs.

The novel focuses on strategies and effective skills to enrich others. Magnetic publishing has an accompanying Program set to run in the spring of 2024. Amanda has over 20 years experience in leadership and sales, she has received numerous awards and continues to serve people all over the world.

A survivor herself of a serious automobile accident in 2010, Amanda continues to teach transformation and embodies a true mindset for adversity at a young age of 36. A Mother, Coach, Author, Advocate, and a True leader. Amanda plans to inspire the world with her passion for writing and serving others.

Chapter 1
~ Leadership As A lifelong Process ~

Amanda M Renaud

I have personally been involved in various leadership positions since I was very young, including grade school. My first experience with leadership was peer mediation and it's where I first developed my passion for finding solutions and leading others.

I spent twenty years learning and growing as a leader and had many unique opportunities and experience. I have always been someone who loves to help others and support others when I can. I found with leadership it is always a learning experience made up of understanding others and their needs as well as the environment and most importantly ourselves. I have written a ton of literature about leadership including my recent publication "Exceptional Minds" which in depth goes into leadership strategies. It has always been a personal interest, and I have grown immensely over the years. My leadership growth did not happen overnight and came with many mistakes and moments of failure. It was one of the most difficult journeys of learning and adapting to life circumstances. In my years of leadership, I've learned a ton and made enough mistakes to know it's always going to be a challenging road ahead.

The Journey of leadership is of full of diversity, changes, and differences. I learned very quickly many leaders have their own styles and execute skills, goals, and overall operations to the best of their knowledge and training available. I've always advocated the need for consistent learning and growth. I have also always been one to really appreciate difference as a learning strategy.

As leaders we have a duty to learn as much as we can so that we can provide the best, latest and most effective skills, mindsets, and strategies to help grow ourselves, our teams, and the people we serve. Leadership is about servitude and not our own ego, needs, and control. It is never about accolades or titles its always about the people we serve and the services we provide.

I've experienced many types of leaders over the decades, including some quite toxic ones but also as I call them "Luminous." Being Luminous when it comes to leadership is about spreading your leadership light and energy bright that others can't help but to admire your contributions and they become inspired and focused to achieve, learn, and grow.

I have often written what it is to be a leader in different perspectives and roles. There are more commonalities than differences in leadership. Adopting attitudes and mindsets to help us connect and resonate with values that align to our style is a critical strategy.

Being a Luminous leader is knowing that your presence and energy highly effects your outcome and the people around you. It is an awareness and understanding about our divine connection to the environments and people around us. Leaders who choose to handle problems with proactively and servitude have the world at their fingertips and are sure to achieve and outperform any challenge.

Luminous Leaders

It takes a level of awareness, discipline, and action to be a truly Luminous leader. Often individuals can get caught up in the tides of challenge, failure, and struggle, this is why not everyone thrives as a leader. With hard work, strategies, training, and perseverance — anyone can thrive as a leader.

I've always believed there are attributes, attitudes and mindsets that help individuals become amazing leaders. The Luminous leader strives for understanding and an ability to learn rather than trying to be right to prove to the people around them they are valid. Luminous leaders understand value comes from the people they serve and the results they can provide for everyone. These luminous leaders vibrate an outward. dedication and commitment to achieve and serve.

When we discuss serving others, I always clarify that; the way we serve others may differ but how we serve others is a shared language.   I personally have noticed over the years a decline in customer service and immense gaps in the workforce are prominent — making it difficult to be a Luminous leader, especially in high stress environments.

Luminous Leadership requires A mindset of that exudes solutions, positivity, and an attitude of servitude. Many never understood why, despite my positions in workplaces I still mopped the floor and did the tedious tasks— I always believed in modeling the behaviors you want your team to have. I have always tried to remain humble and serve my team the best I could no matter what happened or what title I held.

Many times, during my leadership the unexpected would happen and I became better at recovering the situation. If my own mindset was negative, overloaded or I was too stressed — it led to problematic behaviors and poor leadership recovery. Most leaders are fabulous problem solvers, they are creative and want to include the people around them in generating solutions and improving the environment around them by contributing, modeling behaviors, and looking to improve the things around them as much as possible.

Leaders often observe the environment but also take feedback and listen to whatever is being presented to them. Luminous Leaders are effective at communicating and finding unique solutions and ways of meeting goals or getting the job done efficiently.

Sometimes as leaders we won't always hear the best feedback at times, especially regarding rules and operations. I have found that actively listening and taking the feedback to apply it to better solutions, compromise or using the resistance as a teachable moment is helpful.

Luminous leaders tend to make their teams feel empowered and included. I have seen in my many personal experiences what exclusion or alienation can do to a team, and it can end in very poor results and consequences. It seems to happen in some workplaces and can be toxic in nature, team building is a critical skill in a professional environment and is a key indicator of moral character. Leaders who are luminous are excellent at making others feel included and identifying other individuals' strengths. Its always important to tell others their strengths too and offer praise unconditionally.

I have always felt that often we can certainly be quick as humans to jump to assumptions especially around behavior and be punitive when others around us do not meet our expectations or are being insubordinate in our own expectations. I have seen these types of responses often in retaliation instances. Alienation, Isolation, and exclusion is a form of bullying, and it is very damaging to any person.

Luminous Leaders

We know how detrimental it is to be fair, supportive, and inclusive as a leader. A level of emotional intelligence is needed to really execute Luminous Leadership. Leaders who understand the people around them, work hard at building positive rapport and maintain professional boundaries build excellent teams that are cohesive and considerate.

When the leaders are considerate and cohesive the team can also model these behaviors themselves. Teams rely heavily on trust, honesty, fairness, and cohesion. Excellent teams have players that exercise emotional intelligence and awareness to what is occurring around them. These teams and leaders typically aim to express compassion and healthy dynamics that focus on success and goals.

When the leader can create an environment where others around them can be confident, comfortable, and consistent then success is only just a few more steps away. Leaders who share their strategies, solutions and share the success make excellent leaders. Gatekeeping never helped anyone. The people around you are NOT your competition, your poor habits are.

Leaders who give praise, feedback, and build skills make some of the most wonderful leaders there is. Luminous leaders possess an open mind and consider the needs of others always. Being a Luminous leader is all about sharing and spreading all that you know and skills you have. All leaders will struggle and make mistakes, but it is when leaders can be accountable it is always a more respectful light to shine. When leaders create safe environments focused on growth, learning, sharing, and succeeding— others around them can also thrive and succeed.

Good leaders and teams can become lost in toxicity, poor moral, stress and deadlines—it can be quite overwhelming for most. Luminous leaders can recognise when things should be improved, assessed, and revised.

Luminous leaders focus on what they can give to others around them, these are leaders who compromise, actively listen, teach, and support. These leaders shine their Luminous light onto others and consider the needs of their team, environment, and role.

Luminous leaders are both teachers and learners, throughout their journey. Great leaders see people around them as valued, skilled, and teachable. A luminous leader understands that learning is a lifelong process and a continual one at that. The importance of learning is often emphasized with an awareness that developing knowledge, skillsets and experiences is a core value to leadership and success. There is an understanding with luminous leadership that despite the need for more prominent leadership across the country, these leaders often recognise that their journey as a leader is leveraged with the art of servitude and humility.

These leaders see things on a larger scale and understand that serving others is of far greater importance than their own self- motivated desires and ego. Luminous leadership requires the need to build lasting relationships that offer support, authenticity, and acceptance regardless of where the people they serve are in their journey. Being a luminous leader comes from a strong sense of understanding that individuals are diverse, unique, and able bodied to achieve anything when given the right tools, opportunities, and environments. When we often think of leaders who make impact, we can consider their ability to really look at things at a deeper level.

Leaders who are luminous often shine their light onto situations and individual who are not seen. Good leaders often spend a portion of time observing and strategizing to meet large scale goals and accomplishments. Leaders who are definitive on their purpose, goals, and message to others around them — are sure to only enhance their impact and succeed.

Luminous leaders are not afraid of feedback and collaboration because they see the value in a strong foundation and consider teamwork a critical part of their foundation. Collaborations and networking are so important. Luminous Leaders view success as a shared duty and are empowered when others around them are thriving and succeeding.

The luminous leader avoids competitive mindsets and actions. Most competitive attitudes come from a place of ego. Ego focused mindsets and motives always end up becoming a barrier or hindrance to overall success because they are self serving and only seek to fulfill elements that do not often align with the goals of the entire team. Luminous leaders create other leaders and do not hold them back based on their competitive nature or past mistakes. Ego often ends up being a huge hindrance and does not represent an attitude of servitude because it lacks compassion, humility, and self-awareness. Ego based mindsets can often be distracting to others do not meet the needs of others because that mindset indulges profoundly on self motivated desires and actions.

Luminous Leaders strive to possess attitudes and behaviors that are self-aware, and servitude focused. Being aware of how we show up for others can make huge difference in meeting others needs and working toward goals Leaders who have had internal dialogues that are honest and consider how their presence impacts the environment and overall outcome of anything they are building or engaging in do better overall.

When leaders choose to focus on building with others while understanding that every individual has unique skills and purpose to contribute, that competitive nature will no longer align with their leadership morality and values. Leaders should always have an awareness that they inspire people and are observed themselves often by others. Leaders should always model behaviors and attitudes that lift others up, inspire, motivate, and support others around them. Leaders have an important role to play in their communities and the people around them.

We have seen in recent years the power of social media and cancel culture leading to changed societal attitudes about scenarios and individuals who have engaged in misconduct. Leaders also must acknowledge that situations, circumstances, and changes do not change our responsibilities in all we do and how we show up for the world around us.

Being a leader is more than a position or title. It is about our habits, how we spend our time and our ability to achieve big goals and succeed based on how hard we are willing to work and how we respond to life around us. The way we inspire others and serve them is also a critical factor in the impact we make. Many leaders fail to recognise the image and message they put out into the world. Leaders can get caught up in lavish lifestyles and public image and often forget that its not about how leaders look on the outside, but rather how they leave the people around them feeling and how they make people feel seen.

Excellent leadership begins the moment that you start recognizing the people around you and celebrating others. When you offer solutions and recognition you begin to build trust with others and a feeling of safety. You, as a leader begin to grow when you focus on the goals, solutions, and needs of others rather than ego, competition, and anything else that doesn't align with the desired outcome or betterment of the people around us.

Overall being a luminous leader requires many attributes and skills that take time to develop and build upon. No leader is made over night. Luminous leaders make efforts in all they do and achieve and recognise the core elements that difference and diversity are our strengths, especially when it comes to leadership.

Difference and diversity allow for highly skilled and competent individuals to work together to grow together and create wonderful achievements. The differences amongst one another allow for to work together meeting common goals and aspirations. These two very critical core components to leadership demonstrate the need for collaborative, unique and innovative contributions in all corners of leadership and team development.

Leadership and its effectiveness to carry out successful innovations and goals is most profoundly impactful when we as leaders understands we can not know everything or be good at everything. Recognizing that one of the core components to being a luminous leader is using your wisdom to serve others while motivating others to take action and use the actions, skills, and wisdom to apply strategies and solutions that empower others around you to be excited about leadership.

Leadership often intimates some with added responsibilities, expectations, and tasks. Part of being a luminous leader is empowering others to want to be involved and be excited for growth. Believing in your team and the people around you can make a huge difference and intense impact.

Teams who feel confident, valued, and included will begin to want to participate in environments where learning is valued, and mistakes are apart of that learning process.

Luminous Leaders

Leaders who provide safe environments that are positive and impactful always do well with accomplishing their goals. Luminous leaders truly value the learning process and are proactive in nature.

Being a leader is a huge responsibility but the rewards of being able to support others and have the honor of serving others is a gift. There will be many moments you will share with others that will moments of inspiration, clarity, and the start of many wonderful connections.

Luminous Leaders ensure that they are accountable and have a strong sense of compassion in all they do. In my many years, I have met and worked with amazing leaders who have taught me about myself and the world around me. Having a strong network of leaders around you is the ultimate reward and privilege.

Building lasting connections that challenge us, teach us, and help us grow is one of the most rewarding parts of leadership. Understanding that every opportunity has potential to flourish into something that others can also grow from.

Luminous leadership to me will always be about being a leader people can count on, learn from, and grow with. I believe many play leadership roles everyday whether they are informal or formal —it always teaches us valuable lifelong lessons.

~ May Baydoun ~

May Baydoun is an accomplished life coach and ThetaHealing Practitioner. Her purpose is to empower women in business to overcome energetic blocks and limiting beliefs, enabling them to grow their businesses and find balance in their lives. May's entry into coaching and healing is a deeply personal journey, motivated by her life as a small business owner and mother, which inspired her commitment to self-discovery and empowerment.

With a Bachelor of Science in Kinesiology and Exercise Science and a Doctor of Naturopathy (ND) from the College de Naturopathie du Quebec in Montreal, May integrates her extensive knowledge of naturopathy, kinesiology, and alternative therapies into her practice.

May is passionate about making transformation accessible to all, believing that everyone should have the opportunity to thrive. Through her work, she offers guidance and support, helping others create their most fulfilling lives. Her dedication to helping others live with ease, grace, and flow is at the heart of her mission, and she invites clients to join her on a transformative journey to unlock their full potential.

~ May Baydoun Contact ~

Connect with me Below:

Email: may@ascendholistichealing.com

Website: https://ascendholistichealing.com

LinkedIn: https://www.linkedin.com/in/maybaydoun/

Facebook: https://www.facebook.com/may.baydoun

~ Chapter 2 ~

~ We Are All Leaders ~

May Baydoun

I can recall the moment that I realized I was a leader very vividly. I can not say it was a great big event that suddenly threw me into the role of a leader. As a matter of fact, I wanted nothing to do with leadership, being a role model, or managing anyone. All I wanted to do was to live my happy, and quiet life. I wanted this for myself, husband and two daughters.

Much like the quiet life I longed for, my call to leadership came in the most subtle of ways and pulled so hard at my heart strings that there was no way to ignore it. I can genuinely say that in the past, my life was relatively happy. And it was as quiet and peaceful as life could be with two toddlers. I found though that; on the inside, something was bothering me. Something didn't quite sit well despite having everything I had wanted. I had a house to call home, with a big backyard, an amazing husband, as well as two beautiful and healthy daughters. Life was good but I felt so very unfulfilled.

I was working as a realtor at the time from home completing tasks during the day, while my kids were in daycare. I often found myself frustrated that work took me away from my children during evenings and weekends while they were at home, when most people are available to visit homes. I remember telling my girls that they had to play quietly or that I couldn't play with them while they were home. The reason was always because "mommy has to work."

One day, I sat at my desk in the basement, where I was working. My daughters were playing with their dolls, shopping cart, cash register and purses full of play money. That's when I heard the three little words while they were playing that would transform me and my approach to life forever. My oldest daughter, Shireen, at barely three years of age, pulled her little purse up on her shoulder and said to her little sister Shahrzad:" I am going to…just like mommy!"

I looked up, my eyebrow raised, head tilted to the side. Time had stopped. I can not remember what she had said exactly. I could have been going shopping, going to work or cooking. It didn't really matter. I was hooked by the last three words she spoke: "just like mommy." Those words hit hard. It felt like when a cartoon character gets hit on the head by a frying pan. Like an epiphany that strikes as a bolt of lightning. These two beautiful girls of mine, with so much potential and possibilities, with their whole lives ahead of them, will always end up being "just like mommy."

A quick look at my own life confirmed it. I was just like mommy. In more ways than I had liked to of admit. Equally in her beautiful qualities and her less agreeable flaws, I was just like my mommy. And just like she was the example of what a woman's potential could be for me when I was growing up. I would embody that same example for my own daughters as they grew up. I was their role model — I would always be. I did not need to reflect very long on the kind of role model I was being modeling. I had come to the conclusion that I needed to make some changes to improve. I wanted to be a positive example of a woman's full potential. I wanted to be at the very least, able to guide them to reach their own full potential in their own lives.

In that very moment in time, triggered by only three simple words, I understood that my children would never seek to reach their highest potential if I was not willing to do it myself. Children don't do what they are told, they do what they are shown. As their mother, I felt it was my responsibility to show them what is possible. How far a woman can go and all the amazing things she could achieve. I understood and made the commitment to become the very best version of myself that I could possibly be. For my children's well-being, I needed to learn to lead by example. And so, that day, a leader awakened.

The dictionary defines leadership as the action of leading a group of people or an organization. The action of leading means to cause or influence someone to do, or believe, or go along with something.

Easy enough to understand! Dictionary definitions offer a great foundational meaning to words, but do not really highlight the broad embodiment of those words in every day, physical application to life itself. Much like success has a "dictionary definition" and still looks very different in the lives of everyday people, leadership can also take on a large variety of meanings.

I truly believe that every single human on this earth is a leader in some way, shape or form. Many are asleep at the helm, much like I was before my daughter jolted me awake. Some will never awaken to their leadership role and that is perfect for them. Others will boldly step into the leader's persona, impacting many lives and changing the world. And that is perfect for them too.

Regardless of where you might be on the "leadership awareness spectrum," believe me when I say, you are a leader! You may not be the corporate leader at the head of a large enterprise, you may not be a great political leader, or an activist on a mission to create massive change in the world. As a matter of fact, you may be just like me. A more subtle leader, doing small simple things, that compounded, amount to extraordinary shifts in the lives we touch.

Luminous Leaders

There is so much more to leadership than its more commonly accepted ideology. Not all leaders are world renowned, or well known, or even at the head of an organization. But all leaders have an impact on others and create change. Aligned leaders, are the ones who bring a positive influence upon the world around them.

Let us first scratch the idea that there are good leaders and bad leaders. Good and bad are simply a perspective and a matter of opinion. Let us instead make use of the words aligned or misaligned. An aligned leader will lead with the intention of elevating others to their highest potential. A misaligned leader will not always hold that same intention. It's important to keep in mind that people will follow the most aligned leader. They will not follow the leader that aligns with them at that time. I will even venture to say that people will follow a leader that aligns with them, until they outgrow that leader.

Leadership is something you grow into. And very often you will find yourself taking on a leadership role because you care enough about someone else to help them become the best they can be in their life. Much like I voluntarily stepped into the role so my children could have a better life with more opportunities and possibilities than I ever did. I didn't have a clue of what leadership involved, or how to be a leader. I just knew I had to do it.

As comfortable as I was being an introvert, hiding behind a computer screen, with very few friends and not much interest in social gatherings, my kids needed a better example of what they could be, that ultimately meant that someone had to show them what was possible. So, I did what any other mother would have done: I set out to become the very best role model I could be for them.

Luminous Leaders

I think the first key to leadership is that leaders are role models. They give us an idea of the roles we can play. Whether these roles are within our family, our job and career, or within society at large, we model the people we idolize. Awakening to the reality of your leadership role can raise many questions for you. To a certain extent, which is normal. The important thing is that you do not allow your uncertainties to paralyze you with unfounded fears.

I recall my predominant question — after I realized I was a leader to my children — being: "How do I do this?" I had absolutely no clue. Much like when I had my first baby, I had no idea how to be a mother. Sure, I had plenty of advice and support from the nurses at the hospital, my parents, my husband, my extended family. But at the end of the day, I was this child's mother, and I was going to be for a long time. So, I had to figure it out. More importantly, I had to figure out how to authentically be my baby's mother. This meant being true to myself as I cared for her. Leadership is no different. You will not be able to authentically lead anyone if you follow everyone else's way of leading. You will have to figure out what works for you. However, there are some key things that will set the foundation for you to grow into your leadership role with more ease, grace, and flow. Firstly, hold a safe space.

People will always gravitate towards those they know, like and trust. And if you want to be the kind of leader others look up to and come to when they are in need of guidance, you will want to create a safe space where they can feel safe, heard, and valued. This is a concept I learned from mentor and leader extraordinaire — Lisa Nichols. I have applied it in every aspect of my life and the results have been magical.

A safe space is an environment where each party can have a conversation, they feel free and safe to communicate authentically. They communicate without censoring themselves, because there is: No judgement, no repercussion and unconditional love.

Let's break it down! no judgement means that no matter what someone is sharing with you, what you think of them will not change. The greatest attribute any leader can develop is the ability to remain neutral and accepting of everyone as they are, where they are and with all the good, bad, and ugly.

No repercussions means that no matter what is said, shared, or done, there will be no negative consequences for anyone. Not to their reputation, not to their self-esteem, not to any aspect of their life. If you want to be trusted as a leader, you must keep what is shared with you confidential. This is especially true with children, teens, or anyone for whom you are in an authority position. Negative consequences, regardless of their nature or intended purpose, never yield positive results. People already know where they went wrong. Honour their trust in you by showing understanding, compassion, and discretion.

Unconditional love means that you will love them at their best, at their worst and at their ugliest. Every single human being on this earth wants to be loved for the human being that they are. As an authentic leader, you want to be able to genuinely love your people for who they are. Whether they are soaring or struggling, succeeding, or failing, thriving, or getting on your very last nerve, your love for them as the human they are should never waiver. This comes easily when it comes to our own children. It should be the same for our friends, colleagues, employees, acquaintances, and anyone else we encounter. We all could love others unconditionally and a leader makes this common practice.

Hold space for those who look up to you, those who seek your help and guidance and those towards whom you have a certain level of responsibility. Everyone has a journey to navigate and is at a different place in their journey. When you hold space for others, you not only allow them to be who they are and where they are at, you are able to meet and help there. Be a guiding light in their journey.

The role of a leader is to be a beacon for those traveling on the same path, but just a little further behind. We all travel many paths in a lifetime. Playgrounds and playdates, studies, learning to drive, careers, spirituality, travel, retirement, and the list goes on. For every new adventure we experience, someone will be experiencing it at some point. This is truly where a leader can shine, to be of service and to positively impact others.

The magic in leadership is in the capacity to guide others as they navigate their own journey. This is not to be confused with advising or counseling. When we give advice or counsel, we are in essence sharing with someone how we would do something if we were in their shoes. It stems from our level of knowledge, understanding and experience of the world. This doesn't mean that the person receiving our advice or counsel is able to receive it from that same level of knowledge, understanding and experience. People can only perceive things through their own lens. This means that a learning curve is required. A growth curve if you will.

The beauty of being a guide for others is that you can meet them where they are on their path because you have walked that same path. You allow them to make the decisions and call the shots. As a guiding light for others, your role is to illuminate the possibilities and allow them to make their own choices. No one likes being told what to do, or what they should do. Few really care what you would do in their place. The fact of the matter is you are not in their shoes, you are not walking their path right now and you don't know what's best for them. Only they do.

From what I have come to understand, the best way to guide those you have taken under your wing is to empower them by really listening to their story, understanding where they're at and guiding them to find their own solutions and make their own choices.

People often have come to me for guidance. My children, family, friends, and of course coaching clients. With clients I am always sharing wisdom — my knowledge, understanding and experiences — allowing them to draw their own conclusions and make their own choices. With family and friends, it's very different, especially when it comes to my children because I am in a position of authority. It's a very delicate power dynamic in which I want to preserve their freedom to make their own choices for themselves. The first thing I tend to ask when a friend or family member approaches me with something going on in their life is whether they want my perspective or if they just want to talk — aka vent. This makes my role in that moment very clear and avoids either one of us getting frustrated with how the conversation is going.

When all is said and done, I believe the leader's role in the lives of others is to offer seeds of possibility. It's up to each individual to decide if they want to plant those seeds. The guidance a leader offers is simply possibilities. Eye-opening, mind-expanding possibilities. It's about showing the way, helping them up when they fall and letting them soar higher than they could have ever imagined.

Every leader is first and foremost an example of what is possible and achievable. A leader sets the stage, ponders, and collaborates with the team. A leader is not afraid to roll up their sleeves and get their hands dirty. That is what makes them relatable to others. This holds true whether you are a corporate leader, a team leader, a camp counsellor or a mom or dad, aunt, or uncle, setting an example for those you interact with. Relatability is key in building a bond of trust in the relationships you have with those you lead.

Let's face it, no one likes being told what to do or how to do it. Most people will dig their heels in. Almost absolutely everyone is open to being shown new things, new ways, and new strategies. We are all on a journey of learning, growing, and expanding, and we naturally seek and gravitate towards those who can show us the way. Whether we work closely with a leader, for instance on the same engineering team, or from a distance, like following a thought leader on social media, we seek those who can show us the way.

There is an unwritten expectation for leaders to be able to walk the talk. This is the essence of leading by example. It's always easier to follow the lead of someone who has at some point walked the same path or similar. So, as a leader, you must be willing to share your story and share the path you've been through. Not only does it make you more relatable, but also more likeable and trustable. That is the very foundation of relationship building.

As a leader you must be willing to go backwards and get your hands dirty. It's not because you are now in the leadership position that you get to wash your hands clean of all the work you've put in getting to where you are. Sometimes, getting down and dirty with those you lead is the greatest gift you can offer them.

My friend owns a car body shop. Let's call him Rez. His employee, a car body builder with many years under his belt, is an expert at his craft. When the body shop got too busy for just one person to be working on the cars, Rez looked to hire more help. Unfortunately, he couldn't find someone who really fit the team. So, with his very little body work experience, Rez rolled up his sleeves, asked his expert to teach him, and got to work on the cars.

Now this, is brilliant leadership! On one hand, it demonstrates to the employee that the boss has an interest in his well-being and the well-being of the business. On the other hand, it shows that being at the head of a team or company doesn't exclude or excuse a leader from going back to help the team. After all, leadership is about the support we can give others we interact with.

My own greatest lesson in leadership has been learning to step out of someone else's shoes, put on my own heels and walk my own path. It was in 2018, that I volunteered myself to take on one of my most challenging leadership roles. A networking group that I had been attending monthly was at its last lunch event before summer break. The founder of the network announced that she would be stepping down to pursue other projects and passions. The founder called on anyone who might be interested in taking over to reach out to her.

Coincidentally, that same day, I had just mentioned to my partner how I would love to have my own network, but that I didn't want to become competition to the network I was a member of and loved so dearly. I felt it would be somewhat of a conflict of interest. The synchronicities were obvious and the idea that I would go on without this network of amazing women entrepreneurs saddened me. I needed this network and its lunch meetings to continue. So, I reached out. I took notes. I learned how she did it, after summer, I took over.

I did my very best to keep things the way they were. Firstly, because I didn't want to ruffle any feathers, and secondly, I wanted the members to stay with the group. It was, after all, our group. Right? It just wasn't working. Attendance was on the decline. I got to the point where I was the only one showing up for lunches. I hit my breaking point and spent the summer of 2021 going back and forth on the idea of shutting down the network. In the end, I decided to give it one more shot. From September to December… Then, I would re-evaluate. However, this time, I was doing it my way!

I started by scrapping the membership fee and attendance fee. That freed me from the obligation to provide value. I turned it into a casual lunch with the girls who all happened to be women in business. I picked a restaurant I enjoyed where the group was always welcome, no matter how many we were. I automated the invitation and event set-up process. And I showed up to have fun. And just like magic, the network started to grow with new and old members.

The struggles to lead this group taught me one of the most valuable lessons in leadership I could have gained. Authenticity. How to lead authentically, my way and being true to myself and in full alignment with me. Here's the thing… You can't lead the way someone else does, you are not them. You can't walk in their shoes because their shoes have been molded to fit their feet, not yours. You must find your own leadership shoes. And that might mean trying on a few pairs. There will be trial and error. It's inevitable! It's the only way to really figure out what works for you and what doesn't. Ultimately, no matter what you do, you need to be true to yourself. A big part of being true to yourself is discovering who you truly are. This is done with some soul searching and some personal growing. You must understand that there is no such thing as a top tier leader.

You don't just become a leader and stop there. Leadership is an ongoing journey of personal growth and evolution. There's no finish line and no end to how good of a leader you can be. The key to great leadership is that you must become the best version of yourself if you want to bring out the best leader you can be.

A leader's growth never really comes to an end. No one's growth ever really comes to an end. That's the real beauty of our human life. I believe that leadership is the journey of a lifetime. Firstly, because whether we like it or not, whether we want it or not, we are all leaders in the making. It's part of our story. We grow into the role as we grow and evolve as human beings and as our understanding of life expands. Secondly, because leadership becomes a natural part of who we are. It becomes part of our character, our mindset, and our being. Leadership becomes so deeply rooted in so many aspects of our being that it is impossible to one day stop being a leader. That's because we can only evolve, we never devolve.

I hate to be the one to tell you this, but I'm going to tell you anyways: You can't quit being a leader. Leadership is in your DNA. Even as a senior in the glorious, golden years of your life, there will still be someone who looks up to you and seeks your wisdom and guidance. Viewed from this perspective, you don't really get to choose whether to be a leader or not. Being one is simply part of you. We are all leaders.

Where your choice truly lies, is in what kind of leader you want to be. Awakening to the fact that you are a leader is only one part of the equation and only the start of your journey. The rest is about becoming. Becoming the kind of leader, you want to be to those you want to lead. Becoming the best version of a leader, you can be. That means becoming the best version of yourself that you can possibly be. To do that, you need to learn from other leaders, work on your own blocks and limitations, know where you are going in life and as a leader, make a plan to get there and finally, make the necessary course corrections along the way.

Let's dive into these steps and strategies to elevate your inner leader game! While we are at it, allow me to clarify that there's no obligation to become the best leader out there, nor to become the best leader you can be. This will happen organically as you move through your life's journey and as you grow and evolve in your own mindset and way of being. The idea here is to amplify the process and accelerate your leadership journey. Accelerating through such an internal transformation can only lead to an accelerate transformation.

This quite likely will benefit you far more that it will benefit those you lead. Ultimately, the choice to dive in is yours to make…All Right! Back to the topic at hand! Every leader needs a leader. This is an undeniable truth that applies to so many professions, specialties, and skills. Every doctor needs a doctor, every coach needs a coach, every hairdresser needs a hairdresser, and every leader needs a leader. What this means is that you need someone you resonate with, who is where you are headed on your journey and from whom you can learn.

When my own conscious leadership journey began, I was looking for success. That's when I found my local moms in business network and became deeply inspired by the female leaders of that community. In some ways, many of these women were where I wanted to be. Although I didn't work with any of them directly, I did pay very close attention and took notes when those who I most resonated with spoke and offered nuggets of guidance and advice.

When I was introduced to "The Secret" by Rhonda Byrne, I found that I deeply resonated with some of the speakers, but not all. Those who most caught my attention were Bob Proctor, Mike Dooley, Lisa Nichols, and Joe Vitale. The idea that such great leaders would indeed become my mentors seemed foreign. However, in truth, may great leaders teach and lead by example through various avenues and on social media platforms. Naturally, I sought these leaders out and began learning from them. As they shared their perspectives, understanding and points of views, I learned from it and began to transform. As if by osmosis, their ways of being and leading were transferred onto me and I started to change. So did my life. I have found that as I have grown, my mentors have changed. It really is a wonderful thing. It's important to remember that we all have a different journey, different interests and different intentions and goals. Following one mentor from the beginning of our journey and throughout makes no sense. You're a different person so naturally, your path will differ from theirs.

Generally, I will follow a leader for the time it takes me to learn what I need to learn to level up. When this happens, the Universe has usually already sent me my next guide on my journey. I still continue to follow the leaders of my past. However, I always remain open to the new leaders that come my way. I advise you to do the same. Always follow those you resonate with. Take what rings true to you and leave the rest. When a new leader that aligns even more with the new and upgraded version of you shows up, don't hesitate, take the leap! That's the Universe guiding you on your journey.

A word of caution, your journey to phenomenal leadership mastery will not be without bumps in the road. You can expect to come against your own limitations. It would be somewhat foolish to believe that such a journey of personal growth and betterment would be smooth sailing from beginning to end. You are bound to navigate some stormy seas. Challenges are inevitable. They are the catalysts of change and transformation. So, remember, when you find yourself triggered along the way, that it is those very triggers that are your greatest opportunities for growth and transformation.

As a leader, you want to work on your blocks. Not necessarily to overcome them, but rather to resolve them. Believe me when I say that sweeping them under the rug, so to speak, will do you no good. It only keeps you stuck where you are. Stagnation is not conducive to the growth of a leader. A leader evolves through the limitations that present themselves. After all, we attract all thing that present themselves in our lives, be they perceived as good or bad.

This means we attract our own limitations, our triggers, and our blocks. I have come to understand that if something is showing up in our life, then we are gaining from it. It holds a hidden benefit for us. It serves us in some way. Usually, it is either protecting us from something, motivating us for something or justifying and explaining something. Uncovering the hidden benefits of our limitations allows us to draw the lessons to be learned from them and to ultimately understand that we can have the benefit without necessarily having the block or limitations. I use a simple, but powerful journaling exercise to help me resolve my own limitations. I encourage you to use pen and paper rather than screen and keyboard to allow your deeper consciousness to open.

Luminous Leaders

Go through the following prompt questions in order:

Where or how are you feeling limited or stuck?

Where is this coming from?

What is the hidden benefit? How does this serve you?

What are you learning from this?

Are you done learning these lessons?

Can you have the benefit without the limitation?

Are you ready to let this go?

Very often, once lessons are learned, there is no longer any need for the limitation. You can therefore move past it and go forward on your journey. To truly move forward in life, you need to know where you are going. Without a destination or an end goal in mind, you might find yourself going around in circles. One of the most appealing traits of leaders and what entices others to follow their lead is that they always seem to have it together. Whether they do or not, we will never know. However, what gives the impression that they have it all figured out is that they are clear on where they are going. They have a goal in mind, and they are constantly working towards it. There's no time for chaos and disorder in their lives because their mind is focused on their success. They are constantly working towards their success and constantly moving closer to it, they feel successful. That is the energy that we as their audience pick up on.

Getting clear on where you want to go in life is an exercise that only you can do for yourself. I can tell you from personal experience that when I wasn't sure of what I wanted in my own life and didn't have a clear vision for my future, I stagnated. It felt like I was spinning my wheels and running in a rat race without an exit.

A vision for your future is an integral part of your growth. If I may suggest, start with the vision of who you want to be as a leader. You can come back and run through the process again for any other aspect of your life.

As a first step, you are going to write your own definition of what it means to be a leader. The foundation of your vision is based on what leadership and being a leader means to you. This is different from the dictionary definition and can be radically different from one person to another. Much like success means different things to different people, leadership also means different things to different people. It is important to find your own definition. One that makes sense to you and fits your life. You may want to pick up your pen and paper and journal through the process.

Your second step is the vision itself. Project yourself into your future. This could be as far out as you like. My personal preferences are either one year out or December 31 of the current year. It really depends on how much time is left to the year.

The choice really is yours to make. The question to journal on here is: Who are you as a leader in your protected future? Make this detailed. It is the vision of your future self that you are creating. Let your imagination run free! You do, however, want to keep it believable. I encourage you to stretch a little bit beyond what you might think is attainable. However, you mind still needs to believe it's possible for you to get there.

Thirdly, you need to anchor your vision. This is commonly known as your" why" and it needs to be SOLID. You see, having a vision is the destination towards which you are headed. Your "why" is the fuel that gets you there.

If you remember, when we discussed limitations and blocks, we talked about the hidden benefit and how they serve to either protect, motivate, or justify us. The hidden benefit is the "why" to our limitations. It's the reason our subconscious mind holds on to the limitation. When it comes to your goals and your vision, your "why" is the hidden benefit. What do you get out of being the leader you want to be? You're going to need to go deep with this. It's not always so obvious.

Back when I decided to become the best version of myself that I could be, my "why" was a motivational one. I was motivated to be an example for my daughters because I wanted to give them every possibility at success. That "why" was a non-negotiable for me. Your "why" should be non-negotiable.

The last step to the process is to take action towards becoming the leader you want to be. This doesn't have to be massive action, but it does have to be consistent. Taking a course and then leaving the books forgotten on a shelf won't move you to your goals as much as reading a page of a book on leadership daily and implementing your learnings into your life. I encourage you to choose one small thing that you can do daily, that will help you grow on your leadership journey.

Additionally, you will want to reverse engineer an action plan that keeps your vision at the forefront of your mind and allows you to make the necessary changes as you move forward on your journey. Start with your one epic goal. This is the goal that once achieved, all or most of your vision has become a reality. My vision for my leadership journey is to become an international thought leadership speaker. My epic goal is to speak on an international stage with other great thought leaders and mentors from my past.

Once you have determined your epic goal, it's time to start breaking it down. Pick three goals that you can achieve by the end of the current year. You then break your goals down further into three things you can achieve in the next quarter. Then break that down into three things you will achieve in the next month, and three you will achieve in the coming week. As time moves forward, you evaluate and re-evaluate your progress and set your new goals for the coming week, month, quarter, or year.

As you move forward and set your new goals, take a moment to take stock of what you have achieved, how far you've come, what you need to let go of, what you need to move to the coming period and if your goals still apply. This is the perfect time to make any necessary course corrections.

Life is organic and so is your leadership journey. This means that as you grow and evolve so does your life. And as your life grows and evolves, so do your vision and your goals. What you want today may no longer be what you want three months down the line. What you anticipate you can achieve this year; you might achieve in only eight months. What you think will get done this week might not happen because other priorities came up. All of this is okay. It's part of life being an organic thing that flows in its own way and at its own rhythm.

Luminous Leaders

This is where course corrections become important. You get to be honest with yourself about your goals and objectives and whether they still hold true for you. If they do, great! Keep going. If they don't, also great! Set some new goals or change up your whole vision if you like. Ultimately your leadership journey is yours to live and navigate. You're in the driver's seat and you get to choose and decide every part of it, every step of the way. Trust that no matter what you choose, how fast or how slow you go, and wherever you find yourself, right now or at any other time, everything is unfolding perfectly for you.

At the end of the day, so long as you know in your heart that you are doing your very best with what you have and where you are now, you are doing great! Enjoy the journey, that's what life really is all about.

~Lisa Rickards ~

Lisa Rickards is a distinguished leader with over thirty years of experience in senior executive and board roles. Her extensive career spans both local and global markets, offering her a diverse perspective on leadership and business. Lisa has successfully collaborated with and worked for multi-billion-dollar corporations and also leading the full spectrum of nine startups, including her own. This journey has allowed her to develop a unique blend of corporate acumen and entrepreneurial spirit.

Beyond her professional accomplishments, Lisa is deeply committed to giving back. She has led multiple optical missions in third-world countries, providing eye care to over 450,000 individuals, and actively serves on the boards of not-for-profit organizations. Her dedication to volunteer work underscores her passion for making a positive impact in the world.

Lisa's leadership is further shaped by her personal resilience. She has navigated life-altering challenges, including the loss of her husband to cancer and surviving a near-drowning incident keeping her underwater for over five minutes. These experiences have given her profound self-awareness and empathy, which are central to her leadership philosophy. She is deeply committed to cultivating transformative environments where teams thrive, individuals unlock their fullest potential, gain the resilience to push forward, and master the art of working smarter.

Luminous Leaders

Lisa resides in Ontario, where she continues to share her insights through coaching and consulting. Her personal and professional experiences offer a compelling perspective on leadership, which she shares throughout this book and her clients.

Lisa also runs a coaching and consulting practice, where she works with individuals and organizations to unlock their full potential. As a Master Certified Business and Life Coach, she brings a wealth of expertise to guide clients through leadership development, personal growth, and strategic transformation.

Connect with Lisa

on LinkedIn

http://lisarickards.com/

~ Chapter 3 ~

~ Leadership Levels ~

Lisa Rickards

Great leadership is both profoundly simple and incredibly complex. The key lies in understanding yourself and your role as a leader, even what type of leader you want to be, as well as grasping the core attributes that define effective leadership and where these are often overlooked. We will look at insights on how and what you do everyday every interaction you have with others impacts their behaviors, either moving them toward your shared vision or, sometimes unintentionally, in the opposite direction.

In this chapter I go into detail through my experience and eleven fundamental truths that I believe every leader must embrace. These pillars are foundational in effective leadership, serving as guideposts for navigating the challenges and responsibilities inherent to leading others and creating extraordinary followers and teams.

Consciousness: Unaware vs. Aware

Most people go through life accepting what comes their way, believing in a so-called destiny. For some, life is a series of events that happen to them, rather than something they actively shape. As a leader, this passive approach won't serve you or your team well. The first step in becoming an effective leader is to bring awareness to your consciousness.

In my view, consciousness operates on two distinct levels:
Unaware Consciousness: In this state, we accept everything
without question. We tend to replay negative events in our
minds, often reinforcing false beliefs. This unaware state can
have a detrimental impact on our present and future,
influencing our self-belief, happiness, and overall health.
Leaders who operate from this level are reactive, allowing
external circumstances to dictate their actions rather than
shaping their own paths.

Aware Consciousness: This is where the magic happens.
Though difficult to achieve initially, once you gain control over
your thoughts and actions, everything changes. Being aware
means catching those negative thoughts and consciously
choosing to replace them with positive ones. It is being aware
of where we are, our environment and who we are with and
what influence and impact they are having on us and us on
them. A leader that is aware is intentional, confident, and
instills belief, motivation, and courage. The act of becoming
aware of what's happening around you and within you can
transform both your life and your leadership. In leadership,
self-awareness enables you to make more intentional decisions,
inspire trust, and guide others effectively.

Throughout this chapter, we will touch on various aspects of
consciousness and presence, both of which are integral to
becoming a great leader.

Being Present in Leadership

Why is being present important in leadership? Simply put, if
you are not fully present and attuned to your surroundings, you
will miss critical cues from those you lead. Leadership is\about
more than just communicating—it's about truly connecting
with your team, understanding how your words and actions
affect them, and adjusting your approach accordingly.

Here is an example to consider: You are speaking with a direct report and ask them to complete a task by Tuesday. You promise to finish your part by Thursday. However, as you say this, you notice a subtle eye roll. This small gesture might indicate that you've let them down in the past with missed deadlines. A present leader would pick up on this cue and address it immediately, saying something like, "I noticed you rolled your eyes—have I missed deadlines before?" By confronting the issue directly, you can rebuild trust and ensure you follow through on your commitments.

Leaders who fail to notice these subtle cues risk damaging their relationships and eroding trust further.

Another aspect of being present is actively seeking feedback from your team. Once you've established a safe environment (as we will discuss later), you can ask your team directly how you are doing as a leader.

I recommend doing this regularly during one-to-one touchpoints or team meetings. You might ask:

~ **"How do you prefer to be led?"**

~ **"Does my leadership style work for you?"**

~ **"What could I do more of to support you?"**

It's important to remember that leadership is not a one-size-fits-all approach. What works for one team member may not work for another, so flexibility of leadership styles is key. When you ask these questions, be prepared to listen and, if necessary, adapt your leadership style to better meet the needs of your team.

In addition to seeking feedback, getting to know your team on a personal level is crucial. Ask about their goals, both short-term and long-term. Find out what motivates them, what challenges they face, and how you can help them grow. Building strong, authentic relationships with your team requires more than just talking about work. Ask them about their families, pets, hobbies—anything that shows you care about them as people, not just as employees.

Being present also means being open and vulnerable yourself. Leadership is a two-way street, if you want your team to trust you and be open with you, you must be willing to share aspects of your own life, struggles, and growth. Vulnerability creates trust, and trust is the bedrock of strong, effective leadership.

Believe in Yourself and Others

Belief is a powerful force in leadership. The greatest leaders start by showing people why they should believe in them. Once that belief is established, the next challenge is to empower others to believe in themselves.

Self-doubt is one of the most destructive forces a leader can encounter. It occupies prime real estate in our minds, influencing our will, soul, and mind:

Our Will: It's what gets us started, keeps us going, and gives us the resilience to push through tough times.

Our Soul: It's the core of what we believe in, what we live for, and what truly matters to Us

Our Mind: It's the seat of our wisdom, judgement, and intelligence, guiding our decisions.

When self-doubt takes root, it can extinguish your will. The more you hesitate, the more yourself-respect diminishes, until eventually, your willpower gives up entirely. Think about the times you've told yourself, "I'll start tomorrow," only to push that start date further away with each passing day. Every time you delay, your self-belief weakens, making it harder to take action.

Leaders who doubt themselves project that uncertainty on to their teams. People are incredibly perceptive—they can pick up on subtle cues of insecurity or hesitation. If you doubt yourself, your team will doubt you too. But when you believe in yourself and your abilities, that confidence becomes contagious. Your team will trust you more, follow your lead more closely and believe in their own potential because they see your confidence in them.

Combatting Self-Doubt and Cultivating Positive Self-Influence

Self-doubt is a natural part of being human. It's our mind's way of protecting us from potential failure, embarrassment, or disappointment. But while it may have a purpose, unchecked self-doubt can be crippling, preventing us from achieving our full potential. The first steps to overcoming self-doubt is to recognize when it begins to take hold.

One of the most effective strategies for combating self-doubt is cultivating positive self-influence. At its core, self-influence is the conversation you have with yourself. This internal dialogue shapes your confidence, self-worth, and overall well-being. What you tell yourself matters, especially when things don't go as planned.

One strategy I've found effective is not making promises to myself that I have no intention of keeping. Broken promises to yourself erode self-trust, which is the foundation of self-belief. Instead, focus on taking things one day, one step, one thought, and one action at a time. This incremental approach makes daunting tasks feel more manageable and reduces the pressure that often triggers self-doubt. However, overcoming self-doubt goes beyond just keeping promises. It's also about what you tell yourself daily—and, more crucially, what you tell yourself every minute of every day. This is where self-influence comes into play. Consider the times when you've achieved something significant, but instead of celebrating your success, you found yourself downplaying it: "I was just lucky," or "It wasn't that hard, anyone could have done it." This kind of self-talk diminishes your accomplishments and chips away at your confidence over time. On the other hand, when things don't go as planned, it's easy to berate yourself with harsh, negative self-talk: "I'm such an idiot," or "I can't believe I messed that up again." This internal dialogue can be incredibly damaging, leading to feelings of inadequacy, anxiety, and even depression.

At its core, self-influence is the conversation you have with yourself. It's the narrative that runs through your mind when you encounter success, failure, or any of life's myriad experiences. What you say to yourself in these moments matters immensely; it shapes your confidence, your sense of self-worth, and your overall well-being.

Here are some strategies to combat self-doubt and cultivate positive self-influence:

Challenge Negative Thoughts: When self-doubt arises, challenge it. Ask yourself, "Is this thought true? Is there evidence to support it?" Often, you'll find that these doubts are based on fear rather than fact. Replace negative thoughts with affirmations that reinforce your strengths and past successes. Celebrate Small Wins: Recognize and celebrate even the smallest achievements. This practice builds confidence over time and helps to shift your focus from what you haven't accomplished to what you have. Each small win reinforces the belief that you are capable and competent, which benefits both you and your team.

Seek Feedback: Sometimes, we're too close to a situation to see it clearly. Seeking feedback from trusted colleagues, mentors, or friends can provide a more balanced perspective. Positive feedback can boost your confidence, while constructive criticism can help you improve without feeding your self-doubt.

Practice Self-Compassion: Be kind to yourself. Understand that everyone, even the most successful people, experiences self-doubt. Instead of being harsh on yourself for having these feelings, practice self-compassion. Treat yourself with the same kindness and understanding that you would offer a friend.

Visualize Success: Visualization is a powerful tool. Spend time each day visualizing yourself succeeding in your goals. Picture the steps you'll take, the challenges you'll overcome, and the result. This mental rehearsal can help you build confidence and reduce anxiety about future challenges.

Surround Yourself with Positivity: The people you spend time with have a significant impact on your mindset. Surround yourself with positive, supportive individuals who believe in you and your potential. Their encouragement can help you combat self-doubt and reinforce your self-belief.

Focus on Growth, Not Perfection: Understand that growth comes from learning and making mistakes. Perfection is an impossible standard that only fuels self-doubt. Instead, focus on continuous improvement and learning from experiences. This shift in mindset can reduce the fear of failure and help you embrace challenges with confidence.

Take Action: Finally, the most effective way to overcome self-doubt is to take action. Even small steps forward can diminish doubt. When you take action, you gather evidence of your capability, which in turn, strengthens your belief in yourself. The impact of self-influence on your mental and emotional state cannot be overstated.

The way you talk to yourself directly affects your mood, your self-esteem, and your overall outlook on life. Positive self-influence can boost your confidence, increase your resilience, and empower you to take on challenges with a growth mindset. Negative self-influence, however, can do the opposite—it can drain your energy, erode your confidence, and leave you feeling stuck. When you cultivate positive self-influence, it doesn't just impact you; it has a ripple effect on those around you. As a leader, your self-confidence and resilience inspire your team to adopt a similar mindset. Your positive self-talk becomes a model for others, showing them how to handle challenges with grace and determination.

Self-doubt is a formidable opponent, but it's not invincible. By mastering your internal dialogue and adopting strategies to combat negativity, you can weaken self-doubt's grip on your life. Remember, the stories you tell yourself every day are the blueprint for the life you create.

Make sure those stories are ones that empower, uplift, and propel you—and those you lead—toward your greatest potential. And encouragingly to yourself, you're more likely to extend that same kindness and encouragement to others. This creates a culture of positivity, support, and growth within your team or organization. In conclusion, self-influence is a powerful force that shapes your reality. By mastering your internal dialogue, you can transform not only your own life but also the lives of those you lead.

Remember, the stories you tell yourself every day are the blueprint for the life you create. Make sure those stories are ones that empower, uplift, and propel you toward your greatest potential.

Leadership and Self-Belief

Self-Doubt and Self-Influence lead to and impact your overall Self-Belief. So, how does all this apply to leadership? Quite simply, if you don't believe in yourself, how can you expect your team to believe in you, to trust and respect you enough to follow you? The answer is straightforward: they won't. Belief in oneself is the cornerstone of effective leadership, and it's grounded in authenticity and continuous learning Imagine leading a team when you're uncertain of your own abilities or judgment.

That doubt where the journey begins. Leadership begins with cultivating a strong sense of self-belief, will permeate your actions, your decisions, and ultimately, your interactions with your team. People are incredibly perceptive; they pick up on even the subtlest cues of insecurity. If you hesitate, they hesitate. If you waver, they waver. Your self-doubt becomes a mirror that reflects upon your team, causing them to question your leadership and, by extension, their own direction It's often said that you can't pour from an empty cup—you must take care of yourself before you can effectively take care of others. In leadership, this means cultivating a strong sense of self-belief.

This doesn't mean arrogance or blind confidence, but rather a deep, authentic belief in your abilities, grounded in self-awareness and continuous learning. When you believe in yourself, you exude a quiet confidence that inspires trust and respect. Your team feels secure knowing that their leader is someone who knows where they're going and is confident in how to get there.

But let's go deeper. Leadership isn't just about managing tasks or overseeing projects; it's about making a difference. It's about leaving a legacy. This brings us to a more powerful question: "What difference are you trying to make?" Leadership grounded in self-belief isn't just about you—it's about the impact you want to have on your team, your organization, and the world.

When you ask yourself, "What problem am I trying to solve?" or "What is my purpose?" you're aligning your leadership with something greater than yourself. This clarity of purpose not only strengthens your own belief in your leadership but also provides a compelling vision that others can rally around. It transforms leadership from a role into a mission. Consider leaders who have inspired great change. They didn't just lead with confidence; they led with conviction. They knew what they stood for, and they were unwavering in their purpose. Their self-belief was contagious, spreading through their teams and creating a unified force working toward a common goal.

This is why self-belief is not optional; it's essential. It's the fuel that drives your leadership journey. Without it, you're simply going through the motions. With it, you're capable of, guiding, and transforming those around you. Your self-belief sets the tone, establishes the standard, and builds the foundation on which trust, respect, and loyalty are built.

In conclusion, leadership starts with a firm belief in oneself, but it doesn't end there. It extends to the belief in the purpose and vision you carry. It's about making a meaningful difference—one that resonates not only with you but also with those you lead. When your leadership is rooted in strong self-belief, your team will not just follow you; they will believe in the vision you set forth and commit to turning it into reality along side you.

Creating a Safe Environment for Your Team

A safe environment is the foundation of high-performing teams. This is such an important factor in leadership and is more-often-than-not overlooked in its importance and understanding. It's where innovation flourishes, collaboration thrives, truth is set free, barriers removed, and individuals feel empowered to bring their full selves to work. But what exactly does it mean to create a safe environment, and how can leaders cultivate it?

Trust is a cornerstone of effective leadership. Leaders who are trusted by their teams and stakeholders are more likely to inspire loyalty, foster collaboration, and drive sustainable success. However, trust is often fragile and can be easily undermined and lost by actions perceived as unethical or inconsistent.

Feeling Safe: A safe environment is not one where people feel anxious or afraid to speak up. It is not the gut-wrenching feeling of knowing you have something important to say but being too fearful of how it will be perceived. In a safe environment, people are encouraged to speak openly without fear of judgment or retribution. You can foster this by actively listening, valuing diverse perspectives, and creating a culture where all contributions are welcomed—regardless of hierarchy or experience.

Being a leader is admitting when you don't know, when you made a mistake, asking for input and inviting that you build something together, opening the door for others to share ideas, ask questions, and admit mistakes without fear of judgment or retribution.

Encourage Open Communication: Open communication is essential for creating a safe environment. Leaders should strive to build an atmosphere where team members feel comfortable expressing their thoughts, concerns, and ideas. This means actively listening without interrupting, acknowledging the input of others, and responding with empathy, giving credit where credit is due.

Leaders can promote open communication by holding regular check-ins, creating forums for team discussions, and encouraging feedback. It's important to model vulnerability by being open about your own challenges and uncertainties, which signals to your team that it's okay to do the same.

Address Conflict Constructively: Conflict is inevitable in any team, but how it's handled can either strengthen or weaken the team's sense of safety. In a safe environment, conflict is addressed openly and constructively. Leaders should facilitate discussions that allow for different viewpoints to be explored in a respectful manner.

Instead of avoiding conflict, leaders should view it as an opportunity for growth and deeper understanding. By setting the tone for respectful discourse and guiding the team through disagreements, you help reinforce a culture of trust and mutual respect.

Promote Inclusivity and Equity: A safe environment is one where every team member feels valued and respected, regardless of their title, background, or identity. Promoting inclusivity means ensuring that all voices are heard and that everyone has equal opportunities to contribute and succeed. Leaders can promote inclusivity by being mindful of biases, both conscious and unconscious, and by actively seeking to understand and address the unique challenges faced by different team members. This might involve providing additional support, creating mentoring opportunities, or simply being an ally when someone's voice is marginalized.

Support Growth and Development: Creating a safe environment also means supporting your team's growth and development. When team members feel that their personal and professional growth is valued, they are more likely to take risks, be creative, and fully engage in their work.

Leaders should invest in their team's development by offering opportunities for learning, providing constructive feedback, and encouraging continuous improvement. By fostering a culture of learning, you not only help your team members grow but also build a stronger, more resilient team.

Celebrate Mistakes as Learning Opportunities: In a safe environment, mistakes are seen as opportunities for learning rather than failures to be punished. When team members know they can take risks without fear of harsh consequences, they are more likely to innovate and experiment. Leaders should normalize the idea that mistakes are a natural part of growth. By celebrating the lessons learned from mistakes and emphasizing a growth mindset, you create a culture where continuous improvement is not only encouraged but expected.

Lead by Example: Finally, creating a safe environment starts with you, the leader. Your actions, words, and attitudes set the tone for the entire team. By demonstrating integrity, fairness, and empathy, you model the behavior you want to see in your team. Leaders who lead by example build trust and credibility, which are essential for a safe and supportive environment. Show your team that you are committed to their well-being and that you value their contributions. When your team sees that you are genuinely invested in their success, they will feel safe to do their best work.

Back the Team Up: If an idea was given then accepted by you and the team and subsequently taken forward and later does not work out or is challenged by your superior, customer or the organization for any means, it is critical that you do not sell out the team or any individual by diverting blame, questions and attention to them. Any respectable, trustworthy leader would take on any discussions for the team taking on the brunt and protecting any individuals not entering them out.

Take accountability for the decision to move forward with the idea, the consequence of not taking accountability here is trust, you may never get another idea or suggestion again as the team will fear they too will be thrown under the bus, so to speak.

Trust and Ethical Leadership

Incorporating trust and ethical leadership complements our focus on self-belief and self-influence. Trust begins with believing in oneself. Leaders who trust themselves are more likely to inspire trust in others, creating a foundation for strong, cohesive teams. Ethical leadership, on the other hand, is about maintaining integrity and leading with a moral compass. It involves making decisions that are not just right for the business but also ethically sound and transparent. This is particularly crucial in today's complex business environment, where leaders are often scrutinized for their actions and decisions.

Trust and ethical leadership are interdependent. Trust is built through ethical behavior, and ethical leadership is effective only when it is trusted by those it seeks to influence. As the business environment becomes more complex, leaders who prioritize trust and ethics will be better equipped to lead their organizations through both opportunities and challenges.

These principles are crucial not just for achieving short-term success, but for building a legacy of leadership that positively impacts employees, customers, and society at large.

Building Trust Through Self-Belief: Insights into self-doubt are especially relevant here. The connection between self-doubt and leadership is critical: a leader who struggles with self-doubt may find it difficult to gain the trust of their team. On the contrary, a leader who actively works on self-belief, is more likely to be perceived as confident and trustworthy. This trust is essential for fostering an environment where team members feel secure enough to take risks, innovate, and grow.

Creating a Culture of Trust and Ethics: How leaders can actively create a culture that emphasizes trust and ethical behavior. This involves clear communication, setting an example through your own actions, and being consistent in your values and decisions. I pointed out earlier that, self-influence is key here—leaders must model the behaviors they wish to see in their teams. When leaders demonstrate ethical behavior and build trust, it not only enhances their credibility but also encourages others to follow suit, creating a ripple effect throughout the organization, or at home leading by example for your children, siblings or even a significant other.

Building Trust: Trust-building requires leaders to be transparent, consistent, and accountable. It's about aligning words with actions—doing what you say you will do. This consistency creates a sense of reliability and safety among team members, encouraging them to engage more fully and take calculated risks. Authenticity in leaders will aid naturally in gaining trust from followers.

Challenges in Trust: One significant challenge in building trust is the gap between leaders & perceptions of how much they are trusted and the actual trust levels among employees and customers. For instance, many executives overestimate the trust their teams and customers place in them. Addressing this gap requires a close look in the mirror and a deep understanding of the organizational culture that either exists or that you wish to create and the commitment you make to actively earn and maintain trust.

Trust in Hybrid Work Environments: In the context of hybrid and remote work, trust takes on new dimensions. Leaders must manage diverse work arrangements while maintaining a sense of fairness and inclusivity. Trust is critical when employees are dispersed, as it reduces the need for micromanagement and empowers employees to work autonomously. It is also harder to   bond and get to know people as sidebar conversations are awkward and less likely to happen.

Effort must be made here to create meaningful conversations that incorporate all things we have discussed in this chapter. Ethical Leadership: Ethical leadership involves leading with integrity, fairness, and a strong moral compass. Ethical leaders set the tone for the entire organization, influencing the behavior and decisions of others through their own actions. A leader that says one thing and then does another or does not have the courage or energy to do what is required, will be viewed as unethical.

Ethical Decision-Making: Ethical leaders prioritize making decisions that are not just legally compliant but also morally sound. This includes considering the broader impact of decisions on stakeholders, society, and the environment. Ethical decision-making often requires balancing competing interests and navigating complex dilemmas. It is being aware of the broader impact of your decisions. We touched on this in the section on consciousness, we discussed the importance of awareness in leadership. This awareness can be extended to ethical considerations, where leaders must consciously evaluate the potential consequences of their actions on their team, stakeholders, and society at large. Ethics is always about awareness, and self-influence and self-belief and how confidently we navigate challenges while staying true to ourselves, our values, and our people.

AI and Ethical Leadership: As AI becomes more integrated into business processes, ethical leadership involves addressing the ethical implications of AI, such as privacy concerns, data security, and the potential for job displacement. Leaders must ensure that AI is used responsibly and transparently, with clear guidelines on how it affects employees and customers. Corporate Social Responsibility: Ethical leadership also extends to CSR, where leaders are expected to go beyond profit motives to consider the social and environmental impact of their business. This includes promoting sustainability, supporting social justice initiatives, and ensuring that the company's operations contribute positively to society.

The Role of Trust and Ethics in Crisis Management: During crises, the need for trust and ethical leadership becomes even more pronounced. Leaders must navigate uncertainty, communicate openly, and make tough decisions that can affect peoples lives and livelihoods. Ethical leadership during crises involves being transparent about challenges, owning up to mistakes, and making decisions that prioritize the well-being of all stakeholders. I am a true believer in and try to live every interaction with authenticity, be open, be honest, explain the situation.

Most people will understand and accept this far more than a story made up or worse no information at all that leads to speculation, which is usually far worse than any truth.

Empowering your team

To empower your teams is a cornerstone of effective leadership, going far beyond simple delegation. It's about nurturing growth, fostering confidence, and building an environment where everyone can excel. By delegating meaningful responsibilities, leaders help employees hone their problem-solving abilities while equipping them with the skills and training needed for future challenges. Encouraging open communication fosters a culture of collaboration, where ideas are shared freely, and solutions are developed as a team. Recognizing and rewarding achievements not only boosts morale but also fuels continuous improvement.

A clear sense of purpose is achieved through well-defined goals and expectations, while constructive feedback helps individuals understand their strengths and areas for growth. Supporting work-life balance is also crucial in preventing burnout and sustaining long-term productivity. By fostering teamwork, ensuring open dialogue, and demonstrating the behaviors they wish to see, leaders set the tone for a thriving, motivated team.

Empowerment is not just about delegation—it is about creating a space where people feel capable, valued, and inspired to contribute their best. It can also be about being part of something bigger than just the task at hand, or their job, its being part of a team, a vision, a goal, a movement, and them knowing they are a critical part of its success as an individual, but also together as a team.

Motivation & Appreciation

It is hard to trust and respect anyone that does not appreciate you and offer respect back. For one to inspire and lead effectively, creating an environment that nurtures both motivation and appreciation is crucial. Leaders should focus on removing barriers and aligning tasks with employees; strengths, empowering them to find their own motivation. This approach fosters a sense of ownership and prevents feelings of being undervalued.

Luminous Leaders

Additionally, the language a leader uses plays a pivotal role. Encouraging words and clarity during uncertain times not only enhance morale but also boost decision-making and overall job satisfaction. Rather than relying solely on external rewards, leaders should prioritize intrinsic motivators like achievement, growth, and recognition. People thrive when their efforts are acknowledged and when they find personal meaning in their work. Importantly, effective leadership requires understanding that each employee is driven by different factors—whether it's professional development, work-life balance, or a sense of purpose. A one-size-fits-all approach is a recipe for disengagement.

By cultivating a positive, inclusive work environment and encouraging open communication, leaders can minimize conflict and sustain motivation. This ensures employees feel valued, heard, and driven to contribute their best, fueling both individual and organizational success.

Leadership Styles

Leadership is a multifaceted concept, and different styles have emerged to meet the varied demands of organizations and teams. Servant leadership, for example, stands out as a leadership style that prioritizes the well-being, growth, and development of followers over personal goals. Leaders who adopt this approach focus on empathy, stewardship, and building strong relationships based on trust and open communication.

This style fosters environments where learning and reflection are valued, and the leader's role is to serve the team first before leading them toward success. While this approach promotes long-term growth and stability, it can also aid in support from the team when these leaders must balance this approach with the urgency required in high-stakes decision-making and action. In contrast, autocratic leadership is characterized by control, efficiency, and decisiveness. It is effective in situations that demand quick decision-making, particularly during crises or when strict adherence to rules is necessary. However, this style can alienate team members by limiting their input and fostering an atmosphere of obedience rather than collaboration. On the other end of the spectrum, democratic leadership encourages open dialogue and participation from all team members.

By fostering collaboration, creativity, and inclusivity, it can lead to innovative solutions but may also slow decision-making in situations requiring speed and precision.

Transformational leadership is another powerful approach, inspiring followers to pursue a shared vision with passion and dedication. These leaders motivate their teams to push beyond limits and innovate, driving change and improvement. While transformational leadership is highly effective in dynamic and evolving environments, it can create burnout if followers are pushed too hard.

Finally, situational leadership embodies adaptability, as leaders tailor their approach to the specific needs of the situation and the competence of their team members. This flexibility ensures relevance but may sometimes cause confusion if the leadership style shifts too frequently. The key takeaway is that there is no one-size-fits-all leadership style. Effective leaders often must blend various approaches based on the context, organizational goals, and the needs of their teams.

Each style has its strengths and weaknesses, and the most successful leaders are those who can recognize when to apply each one strategically.

~ Maria Rekrut ~

Maria Rekrut: A Brief Biography

Maria Rekrut is a multifaceted entrepreneur, real estate investor, and mentor based in Niagara-on-the-Lake, Ontario, Canada. With over twenty-five years of experience in real estate investing, Maria has established herself as a respected figure in the industry.

As the owner of Real Estate Media, News, Radio, and TV Network, Maria hosts radio and TV shows aimed at educating and empowering real estate investors and landlords. She is also a #1 International Best-selling author, podcaster, and YouTube content creator, sharing her expertise through various media channels.

Maria's journey in real estate began after overcoming personal and financial challenges, which shaped her resilient approach to business and life. Her experience spans various aspects of real estate, including vacation rental investing, which she particularly enjoys and advocates for.

In addition to her real estate ventures, Maria has a background in classical music, having studied vocal performance at the Conservatorio Di Santa Cecilia in Rome, Italy, and pursued doctoral studies in voice at the Escuela Superior Dei Canto in Madrid, Spain.

Throughout her career, Maria has been recognized for her contributions to business and the community. She has been nominated for Businesswoman of the Year by the Niagara Falls Chamber of Commerce multiple times.

Luminous Leaders

Maria is known for her passion for helping others succeed, which is evident in her mentoring and coaching work. She has developed and delivered programs for various institutions, including Niagara College, Brock University, and the University of Manitoba.

As a respected member of the Niagara community since 1986, Maria has served on various boards and committees, including being the only woman Hydro Commissioner in the history of the Niagara-on-the-Lake Hydro Commission. She fought to save the local Hydro Commission from being sold to a USA-based firm. She won that fight!!

She ran for Niagara on the Lake City Council three times; she was driven by the desire to stop unnecessary development and get things organized to help citizens of the town Niagara on the Lake to keep their town historic.

Maria Rekrut continues to be an active voice in the local and Canadian real estate and business development sectors, sharing her knowledge and experience to help others achieve their goals and reach their full potential.

~ Chapter 4 ~

The Brave Mentor: Maria Rekrut's Journey from Adversity to Empowerment

Maria Rekrut's story is one of resilience, innovation, and unwavering determination. Her journey from financial struggles to becoming a successful real estate investor and mentor has not only shaped her own life but has profoundly influenced her approach to coaching and empowering others. This chapter explores how Maria's bravery has become the cornerstone of her mentoring philosophy, inspiring countless individuals to overcome their own challenges and achieve their dreams.

Rising from the Ashes: Maria's Personal Journey

Maria Rekrut's path to success was far from smooth. Following a devastating marriage breakup, she found herself facing significant financial hardships. However, it was during this dark period that Maria's true strength emerged. Instead of succumbing to despair, she chose to view her setbacks as fuel for future success. This pivotal moment in Maria's life became the foundation of her mentoring approach. By openly sharing her story of overcoming adversity, she creates an immediate connection with her mentees. Her vulnerability and authenticity resonate deeply with those who are struggling, offering them a beacon of hope and a living example of what's possible with determination and the right mindset.

Luminous Leaders

Resilience as a Guiding Principle

Maria's advice to "Stay Motivated" is not just a catchy phrase but a core tenet of her coaching philosophy. Drawing from her own experiences, she teaches her mentees to reframe challenges as opportunities for growth. This perspective shift is crucial in developing the mental fortitude required to succeed in competitive fields like real estate investing.

In her mentoring sessions, Maria often emphasizes the importance of developing a resilient mindset. She encourages her mentees to analyze setbacks objectively, extract valuable lessons, and use these insights to fuel their future endeavors. This approach not only helps individuals bounce back from failures but also transforms them into more adaptable and resourceful professionals.

Simplifying the Complex: Making Success Accessible

One of Maria's most significant contributions as a mentor is her ability to simplify complex concepts. Her advice to "Simplify Your Approach" stems from her own experiences navigating the intricate world of real estate investing. Recognizing that overwhelming complexity can often lead to inaction, Maria has developed straightforward investment techniques that are accessible to newcomers and experienced investors alike.

This simplification process is a testament to Maria's bravery in challenging conventional wisdom. By breaking down complex strategies into manageable steps, she empowers her mentees to take action with confidence. Her approach demystifies the often-intimidating world of real estate investing, making it accessible to a broader audience and fostering a new generation of successful investors.

The Power of Perseverance

Maria's journey is a living testament to the power of perseverance. Her advice to "Persevere" through challenges is not just empty rhetoric but a reflection of her own life experiences. In her mentoring sessions, Maria often shares anecdotes from her own journey, illustrating how persistence in the face of seemingly insurmountable obstacles ultimately led to her success.

This emphasis on perseverance is a crucial aspect of Maria's mentoring approach. She teaches her mentees that success is rarely achieved overnight and that the ability to stay committed to one's goals, even in the face of repeated setbacks, is often the determining factor between success and failure. By instilling this mindset in her mentees, Maria prepares them for the inevitable challenges they will face in their own journeys.

Embracing Continuous Learning

In a rapidly changing world, Maria recognizes the importance of staying informed and adaptable. Her advice to "Stay Informed" about global events reflects her own commitment to lifelong learning. As a mentor, Maria encourages her mentees to develop a curious mindset, constantly seeking new knowledge and perspectives that can inform their decision-making processes.

This emphasis on continuous learning is particularly evident in Maria's approach to technology and social media. Despite not growing up in the digital age, she has embraced these tools as powerful assets for business growth. Her book on "Double Your Income Using Social Media" is a testament to her ability to adapt and thrive in changing environments. By leading by example, Maria inspires her mentees to step out of their comfort zones and explore new avenues for growth and success.

The Renaissance Entrepreneur: Inspiring Versatility

Maria's description as a "Renaissance Serial Entrepreneur" is not just a title but a reflection of her diverse skills and interests Maria is more than just a "Renaissance Serial Entrepreneur"; this title truly encapsulates her wide-ranging talents and passions. She has excelled in various fields, including music as a soprano with a doctorate, real estate investing, business consulting firm "Maria Rekrut & Associates. Coach and Keynote speaker and media production. Her diverse accomplishments serve as a source of inspiration for her mentees. Maria actively encourages those she mentors to embrace their full potential by exploring multiple avenues rather than confining themselves to a single career path.

This versatile approach to entrepreneurship is a key component of Maria's mentoring philosophy. She teaches her mentees that success often comes from the ability to adapt and pivot when necessary. By sharing her own experiences in different industries, Maria demonstrates that skills and insights from one field can often be applied successfully to another, fostering a more flexible and resilient approach to business.

Empowering Others: The Heart of Maria's Mission

Perhaps the most significant aspect of Maria's mentoring approach is her genuine desire to empower others. The founding of Real Wealth Real Estate is a clear manifestation of this mission. By creating a platform to share her expertise and experiences, Maria demonstrates remarkable courage in empowering others to achieve their own success.

Luminous Leaders

This commitment to empowerment is evident in every aspect of Maria's mentoring style. She doesn't just provide information; she actively works to build her mentees' confidence and self-belief. Maria understands that true success comes not just from knowledge but from the courage to act on that knowledge. Her mentoring sessions often focus on helping individuals overcome their fears and self-doubts, encouraging them to take calculated risks and pursue their goals with conviction.

The Power of Human Imagination

Maria's emphasis on the power of "Human Imagination" in her presentations reveals another crucial aspect of her mentoring approach. She understands that success often begins with the ability to envision new possibilities. As a mentor, Maria works to unlock her mentees' creative potential, encouraging them to think beyond conventional boundaries and imagine innovative solutions to challenges.

This focus on creativity is particularly valuable in fields like real estate investing, where the ability to see potential where others can not lead to significant opportunities. Maria's mentoring sessions often include exercises and discussions designed to stimulate creative thinking, helping her mentees develop the visionary mindset necessary for long-term success.

Authenticity in Action

Maria's "critically authentic perspective" in her workshops and seminars is a direct result of her bravery in being genuine and transparent about her experiences. This authenticity is a cornerstone of her mentoring approach, creating an environment of trust and openness that allows her mentees to be vulnerable and honest about their own challenges and aspirations.

By sharing both her successes and failures, Maria creates a safe space for learning and growth. She teaches her mentees that authenticity is not a weakness but a strength, allowing them to build genuine connections and foster trust in their professional relationships. This approach not only leads to more effective learning but also helps her mentees develop their own authentic leadership styles.

Fostering Self-Belief: The Foundation of Success

At the core of Maria's mentoring philosophy is the belief that everyone has the potential for success, regardless of their current circumstances. Her own journey from financial struggles to prosperity serves as a powerful testament to this belief. As a mentor, Maria works tirelessly to instill this sense of self-belief in her mentees, helping them recognize and harness their own potential.

This focus on self-belief is particularly important when working with individuals who may be facing significant challenges or setbacks. Maria's mentoring approach often includes exercises and discussions designed to challenge limiting beliefs and build confidence. By helping her mentees develop a strong sense of self-efficacy, she empowers them to take bold actions and persist in the face of obstacles.

Conclusion: The Ripple Effect of Brave Mentorship

Maria Rekrut's approach to mentoring and coaching, shaped by her own bravery and resilience, has created a ripple effect of empowerment and success. By sharing her journey, simplifying complex concepts, encouraging perseverance, and fostering creativity and self-belief, Maria has not only achieved her own success but has also paved the way for countless others to realize their dreams.

Her story serves as a powerful reminder of the transformative impact that brave and authentic mentorship can have. In a world often characterized by uncertainty and rapid change, Maria Rekrut's mentoring philosophy offers a beacon of hope and a roadmap for success. Through her work, she continues to inspire and empower a new generation of entrepreneurs and investors, proving that with courage, determination, and the right guidance, anyone can overcome adversity and achieve their goals.

Maria Rekrut's book "Double Your Income Using Social Media" has become a cornerstone resource for entrepreneurs and business owners looking to leverage digital platforms for growth. As a #1 international best-selling author, Maria draws from her extensive experience in real estate investing and business development to provide practical strategies for increasing revenue through social media engagement.

Double Your Income Using Social Media

The book focuses on several key areas that can help businesses maximize their social media presence:

Developing a Strategic Approach

Maria emphasizes the importance of creating a cohesive social media strategy aligned with overall business goals. She guides readers through the process of identifying target audiences, selecting appropriate platforms, and crafting content that resonates with potential customers.

Leveraging platform-specific features

Each social media platform has unique features and algorithms. Maria provides in-depth insights into maximizing visibility and engagement on popular platforms like Facebook, Twitter, Instagram, and LinkedIn. She covers topics such as optimal posting times, hashtag strategies, and utilizing paid advertising options effectively.

Building authentic connections

A core theme of the book is the importance of authenticity in social media marketing. Maria shares techniques for creating genuine connections with followers, emphasizing the value of two-way communication and community building. She illustrates how fostering real relationships can lead to increased brand loyalty and word-of-mouth referrals.

Content Creation and Curation

Maria offers practical advice on developing a content strategy that provides value to followers while promoting business offerings. She discusses various content types, including text posts, images, videos, and live streams, and how to tailor content to different platforms and audience preferences.

Analytics and Optimization

The book delves into the importance of tracking social media performance through analytics. Maria guides readers on interpreting key metrics and using data-driven insights to refine their social media strategies continually.

Monetization Strategies

Perhaps most crucially, Maria provides actionable strategies for converting social media engagement into tangible business results. She covers techniques for driving website traffic, generating leads, and closing sales through social media channels.

The Magnetic Entrepreneur

Beyond her bestselling book, Maria Rekrut has established herself as a "Magnetic Entrepreneur," attracting followers and clients through her dynamic presence across various media channels. Her approach combines:

Thought Leadership

Maria regularly shares insights on real estate investing, business development, and social media marketing through her blogs, podcasts, and speaking engagements. This consistent output of valuable content positions her as a go-to expert in her field.

Luminous Leaders

Multi-Platform Presence

Recognizing the importance of meeting her audience where they are, Maria maintains an active presence across multiple social media platforms:

- **Facebook:** Maria uses her personal profile and business page to share industry news, tips, and behind-the-scenes glimpses into her entrepreneurial journey.

- **LinkedIn:** Her professional profile serves as a hub for business-oriented content and networking with other industry professionals.

- **Twitter:** Maria leverages Twitter's real-time nature to engage in industry discussions and share quick tips and insights.

- **Instagram:** Through visually appealing posts and stories, Maria showcases her real estate projects and provides motivational content for aspiring entrepreneurs.

- **YouTube:** Her channel features in-depth tutorials, interviews with industry experts, and vlogs documenting her business experiences.

Luminous Leaders

Personal Branding

Maria has cultivated a personal brand that blends professionalism with authenticity. She openly shares her own experiences, including challenges and successes, which helps her audience relate to her journey and trust her advice.

World Renowned Expert

Maria's influence extends far beyond her local Canadian market. Her expertise in real estate investing, particularly in vacation rentals, has garnered international recognition:

Global Speaking Engagements

Maria is frequently invited to speak at real estate and entrepreneurship conferences worldwide, sharing her insights on topics ranging from vacation rental investing to social media marketing for real estate professionals.

International Consulting

Through her business development consultancy, Maria works with clients from various countries, helping them adapt her strategies to their local markets and cultural contexts.

Media Appearances

As a recognized expert, Maria has been featured in international real estate publications and has appeared on global business news networks, further solidifying her reputation as a world-renowned authority in her field.

Luminous Leaders

Ongoing Support for Real Estate Investors

Maria's commitment to empowering real estate investors worldwide is evident in her ongoing initiatives: Real Wealth Real Estate Platform through her website realwealthrealestate.com, Maria provides a wealth of resources for both novice and experienced real estate investors. This includes:

- Regular blog posts covering market trends, investment strategies, and property management tips

. - Webinars and online courses on various aspects of real estate investing, with a particular focus on vacation rentals.

- A community forum where investors can connect, share experiences, and seek advice.

Podcasting and Radio Shows

Maria hosts several podcasts and radio shows focused on real estate investing, including:

- "Maria Rekrut and All Things Real Estate" on the radio station-https://4680q.com/, where she discusses current market trends and interviews industry experts.

- A podcast series on Spotify, dedicated to short-term and vacation rental investing, providing listeners with actionable strategies and insights.

The Real Wealth Radio Station- is Maria's newest project to reach more real estate investors, landlords, and businesspeople worldwide. The tagline for her internet radio station is "Come for The Music, Stay for The Business Advice." **https://realwealthradio.ca/**

Luminous Leaders

Coaching and Mentorship Programs

Recognizing the value of personalized guidance, Maria offers:

- One-on-one coaching sessions for serious investors looking to scale their real estate portfolios.

- Group mentorship programs that combine structured learning with peer support and networking opportunities.

- Mastermind groups for experienced investors to collaborate and tackle complex market challenges.

Real Estate Investors Association

As the founder and president of the Canadian Real Estate Investors Association, Maria continues to organize events, workshops, and networking opportunities for investors across Canada. This association serves as a hub for knowledge sharing and collaboration within the Canadian real estate investment community.

Educational Content Creation

Maria consistently produces educational content across various platforms:

- YouTube tutorials covering topics like property analysis, financing strategies, and renovation tips.

- E-books and guides on niche topics within real estate investing, available through her website and other digital marketplaces.

- Regular newsletters providing market updates and investment opportunities to her subscriber base.

Technology Integration

Recognizing the growing importance of technology in real estate, Maria helps investors:

- Navigate property management software and tools to streamline their operations.

- Understand and leverage emerging technologies like virtual reality for property showcasing and blockchain for real estate transactions.

- Implement data analytics tools to make more informed investment decisions.

Global Market Insights

Leveraging her international network, Maria provides investors with:

- Insights into emerging global real estate markets and cross-border investment opportunities.

- Guidance on navigating international real estate laws and regulations.

- Strategies for building a geographically diversified real estate portfolio.

Through these multifaceted efforts, Maria Rekrut continues to be a driving force in the real estate investment community, empowering investors worldwide with the knowledge, tools, and confidence to succeed in an ever-evolving market landscape. Her commitment to education, innovation, and community-building has established her as not just a successful investor but as a true thought leader and mentor in the global real estate industry.

~ Sammie Lee Hill ~

Sammie Lee Hill, born in San Francisco and raised in North Richmond, California is a retired California Police Officer. After retiring, he attended Saint Mary's College in Moraga receiving a certificate in Legal Studies in 1995. Sammie then began work in Community Relations at Richmond High School. Sammie's primary duties there involved mentoring and counseling students.

Sammie created the educational program, "Student Principal of The Year" which was designed to assist high school seniors prepare for college.

In 1998, Sammie began his acting career in a role as a uniform Police Sergeant on the hit television show, "NASH BRIDGES" starring Don Johnson and Cheech Marin. Sammie wrote the "Mentor Theme Song" that received numerous national and international awards including a letter of praise from former President, George W. Bush.

The song also received recognition from the United State Congress and the State of California. This song later became the official Mentor Theme Song for "Mentoring Appreciation Day" on April 26, 2000.

Sammie has been a member of the American Society of Composers, Authors, and Publishers (ASCAP) since 1998. Sammie's Talent Agent is Steven Bernier of Street Dreams Productions in Oakland, California.

Sammie recently signed a major international music contract for the Mentor Theme Song to be enhanced and recorded by BELINDA, the famous Mexico Superstar Singer. The song will be recorded and performed in English, Spanish and French. The Mentor Theme Song is currently in the process of being endorsed by thirty-two countries.

Sammie is also involved in the development and production of an international documentary entitled "SECOND CHANCE" created by Eric Sanchez. This project is designed to provide educational information to show strokes survivors various paths to recovery that can improve their quality of life.

Sammie recently became a member of SUCCESSWORLD1, COMMONWEALTH ENTREPRENEURS CLUB and the INTERNATIONAL HUMAN RIGHTS COMMISSION.

Agent: Steven C. Bernier, LDA, Phone: +1 (888) 829-3435, Email: sbernier@StreetDreamsProd.com

Contact: Sammie Lee Hill, Phone: +1 (510) 374-0347, Email: samleehill@aol.com

Sammie Lee Hill
~ Honorable Mention ~

In my professional field, I characterize Leadership as the ability to encourage, influence and inspire other individuals to accomplish or achieve a Goal. As a Mentor and Leader, I motivate and encourage innovation in order help others to become positive and productive role models to assist other individuals to manifest their goals. As a retired Police Officer and a former Community Relations Liaison at a Local High School, I have always interacted with high school students to do their best in order to reach and elevate in higher learning. The students are our future Leaders!

Sammie Lee Hill

ASCAP Songwriter

Website: www.thementorthemesong.com

~ Antoine Airoldi ~

Antoine is from Canada, where he is a teacher and Best-Selling Author. Antoine enjoys creating music is his free time and is a father, which keeps him very busy. Antoine also does work in leadership development, Brand consulting, public speaking, and life coaching. Antoine has also developed strong skills in accounting and pricing strategies. Antoine is the owner of Antoine communications Inc which was founded in 2018. Antoine has exceled over the years in his each of his fields. From specializations in teaching to digital marketing, he has become a true leader in all he does. Antoine loves to teach others and is always developing new and innovative strategies and techniques to share with his customers and the people he works with.

http://linkedin.com/in/antoineairoldi.com

www.antoineairoldi.com

1 (514) 515-4041 Phone

~ Chapter 5 ~

Antoine Airoldi

Luminous Leadership in Expeditious Environments

From fleeting refugees to economic crises globally, everyone now lives in a world of hurt. Yet that hurt can cease to exist due to luminous leadership. However, how can such problems disappear?

Of course, they cannot dissolve overnight. It takes strategic thinking and action to get there. By writing this piece of literature — this global problem can have its own isolation — and therefore, can be solved.

Luminous leadership is not meant to be a taboo topic of any sort but rather enlightenment at its best to solve current and future issues, whether political, government, or daily conflicts. And it's easy to use leadership as a buzzword, but it's far from it.

The word leadership has been used in government and corporate settings to distinguish higher-ups and has separated senior and junior positions all to the point of giving meaning to something that may not have meaning in the first place. For example, in a previous role, recruiters were known to be junior positions, and the account executives were the true leaders of the industry.

Luminous Leaders

The issue with this previous experience was that the recruiters had no training to transition to the account executive role. You can already see the issue here. It showed that there was no way of progressing and then leadership was tossed around for the wrong role.

In all fairness, leadership, strikingly as it seems, is in every role. And it has nothing to do with one person being better than someone else. A true leader is on the field, working when no one else. But how can I prove this to be true?

The reason is simple; when I got let go as a recruiter, I decided to chase my passion. And so, I worked as a supply teacher. Day and night, I was working with people and helping people grow. That was when I discovered what being a luminous leader looked like. And I'm sure you may be dealing with a similar conflict? You're maybe climbing the corporate ladder but at what cost?

An unattainable position is an unattainable position, and it may be hurting you and your loved ones. So, let this be your cry for help. If you haven't been 100 percent satisfied, change. Change your job, your environment, your situation. It sounds bold but is worth it. And is freeing. That's what luminous leadership is all about.

It's about making beneficial situations. And you may ask, who decides what luminous leadership is all about? It's yourself, it must benefit you and others around you. You can always point out the decisions you make and how they benefit everyone around.

In my situation, I complained a lot less, I had less corporate stress due to bosses overlooking my every move. However, when I was let go of my previous role, the lack of income played a lot emotionally, until it was gone - and accepted that things would get better under circumstances that are more favorable. Like mentioned above, your perfect situation may not be what you're currently living. While this life of yours may be expeditious, you still have the power to control it.

Don't forsake your choices as you do have control over them. To thrive in this environment is not to simply understand it, but rather control it. You can block, delete, and remove yourself from certain things.

Most digital content nowadays is pure noise and rages towards your attention and well-being. How so, you ask? If it doesn't help you grow, it will hurt you. You can read research and learn new things instead of doom scrolling. As a millennial myself, I've dealt with this, and if you too are one, you know what I'm talking about. Doom scrolling is looking at content and being hypnotized to apps that consume all your attention.

It is very hard to disconnect from as it's where people seek attention and likeability. If you don't, please that crowd, you are less than when it comes to anything. This may sound just as bad as a corporate gig you cannot get out of. These fast-paced environments suck you in at a quick glance.

Leadership in these areas are consistent. The ones with the most shares, likes, money earned is the leader. Consider, do they truly deserve it? That is not for me to decide, but to depict this given subculture, and digital reality most live in. We are all guilty of this to some extent, getting rid of the digital world now is close to impossible.

These cultures make you have a sense of belonging and control to some extent — if you fit in. These subcultures will exist for as long as we are here. Now, the reason cultures like this lack leadership is there are few movements that make sense. And no, a trend or hashtag can't save lives or prevent animals from being extinct, and so forth in my opinion. That's what we call public relations by living in these digital cultures, but they don't solve problems. Only action can.

Moving forward, luminous leadership is best kept in the public with real people that can interact with one another; dissociation from the web or any culture that comes forth would be the best. For leadership to have its full impact, we need real people engaging in a live setting.

In conclusion, we are far better off once we truly live through such intentions and do so in harmony with one another. How many times have you seen a loved one stuck on their phone for no apparent reason? As if the phone and subculture was far more important than what was happening right in front of them. It's real and it exists. Now, how do we prevent it? Luminous leadership is the answer. Now share it with others, so we can get back to what is important. Our connections with one another.

~ Mark Bentcover ~

Who is Mark Bentcover? If you find out let me know. What have I done in my life? Professional musician, actor, engineer, program manager, college professor, CTO, writer, skydiver... blah blah blah.

I have worked for decades in universities teaching hundreds IT, lean manufacturing, Six Sigma, agile development, writing, psychology, and more. I have hired and fired hundreds for Fortune 500 companies as a manager on the factory floor to the executive board room I am currently helping an education development company as a subject matter expert in agile development in general and the Product Owner role specifically.

As I enter the last laps of my professional career, I am looking to pass the torch through sharing my knowledge and experiences to anyone who will listen. My core values include transparency, clarity, directness, respect, and growing the human spirit to help as many people live a rich and fulfilled life as I can. I do this by living and breathing the principles of Servant Leadership.

So, who is Mark Bentcover? These things and more. Living life at full throttle and learning new things everyday in every way. Won't you come join me? Living your best life creates a better world for everyone. So go live your best life, I know I will and am.

Contact Mark Bentcover:

PO Box 85, Cannon Beach, OR, 97110

markyb@eocstudios.com

~ Chapter 6 ~

Mark Bentcover

Leadership Unlocked

A topic which has thousands, if not millions, of words spoken, written, shown about it. Many of these are spent focused on people who as part of their role must manage people or processes in an organization or company. The more philosophical address the nature versus nurture aspect. Are leaders born (natural) or can they be grown (environment/ nurture)? Is the role of "leader" assigned/appointed or gained by the actions and attitudes of a person? Is leadership an art or a science? The answers are simple but not easy:

The aptitude for leadership may vary at one's birth but you can grow into a leader through your education (formal or informal, academic or professional, from another or self- taught/learned), a nurturing environment (surrounded by a person or persons who create a safe space for you to try, fail, learn, as well as be coached and mentored).

In my decades long career (not done yet) or as a friend of mine says "a long time," I have had to be leader in title numerous times. My experience is that less than 25% of people who have "leader" in their title or job description exhibit any leadership. So, I vote for being a leader is defined by how someone acts within the context of an engaging attitude and cult of personality. One caveat here is that no two leaders look or act exactly alike and you must find your own style of leadership.

It is also both an art and a science. The art is the "style" I mentioned earlier. The science is all of the models, tools, and processes that many have spent tomes, papers, presentations, training, conferences, etcetera on attempting to "teach" us what leadership is.

This chapter will try to balance the art and the science by espousing various models combined with examples of how to apply your style (or art) within the context (or even blowing up the models entirely). Too many people leave the art part out of the question of what leadership is. To me the "art" always involves the people whether it be the person trying to be (or being) the leader or the people, teams, or organizations they are trying to lead.

The science is clean (usually), people are messy (and wonderfully so). In a time of economic uncertainty, social unrest, and political upheaval leaders are needed more than ever. Too many of us have been seduced into the superficial division fed by social media founded on the ideas of people who call themselves wise, who have anointed themselves leaders... and the masses have sheepishly let them... followed them...

Be it emotional, intellectual, spiritual, or physical. I can think of no other time in human history when good leaders have been needed more. The famous question posed by George Berkeley (1710) applies to this topic:

If a tree falls in the forest and no one is there to hear it, does it make a sound? The physics' answer is yes because sound is defined by the production of sound waves. The hearing mechanism of people or animals is what receives the sound waves and recognizes them as such. Leadership is similar. A leader is a leader.

Even though they may not be revealed as such unless there are people to follow them, they are who they are. Its like

Schrödinger's Cat... are you a leader? No one will know for sure until you have led someone.

As John Wooden once said: "The true test of a man's character is what he does when no one is watching." This may seem contradictory for the topic at hand. I can only assert what it is not. what someone says to your face and what they do behind your back is the true measure of a leader.

How many of us have been in organizations where our managers glad hands us and tells us what we want to hear in public but then either no action supporting these words occur or...Worse, the opposite occurs (actions or words directly in opposition to what was said and/or promised).

I believe the science of leadership can be divided amongst the 4 Cs. The weird part is that many experts cite 4 Cs, but they are not all the same Cs.

I have always leaned on the original as relayed to me in Peter Drucker's 1939 through 1943 tomes: The End of Economic Man: The Origins of Totalitarianism, The Future of Industrial Man, and Concept of the Corporation. Overall, he saw management, when practiced well, was one of the best defenses against fascism and other government structures which oppress humans. One of his more famous quotes:

"Management is doing things right; leadership is doing the right things." And leadership is management practiced well.

My only caveat is you do not have to be in the role of "manager" or "leader" to manage or lead. As stated earlier many who have these roles are NOT leaders in any shape or form.

Drucker's 4 Cs of Management are: competency, character, compassion, and community. Some alternates are creativity, communication, critical thinking, and collaboration. To me these are skills or practices within the original four. If you have a sense of community and compassion, you will automatically communicate well and collaborate often.

If you have a high level of competency, you have and will exercise creativity and critical thinking. Drucker is also the grandfather of Management by Objectives (MBO). Objectives within the context of the vision, mission, and goals of the organization. Goals being the larger company's aim for the year and objectives being the "goals" of smaller groups and individuals within the company. Drucker believed in Dorat's construct of SMART goals (specific, measurable, achievable, realistic, and time-bound).

In my experience MBO when practiced well is very efficient and effective. The place where organizations fail is by having too many of any of the four horsemen of the apocalypse (VMGO). A vision should short, clear, and motivational. The mission should provide the context within which to accomplish the vision. Goals and objectives are basically performance measures.

To me both the vision and mission should be singular. There can be only one (of each). There can be multiple parts of a mission but should be short and sweet. Annual goals should number between three3 and five as should objectives. In an experiment I ran with the research and development department of a large Fortune 50 company we found that people who had three to five objectives accomplished all of them 90% of the time. Those who had more exponentially accomplished less with ten and greater being the line where most people did not accomplish any of the objectives. In another experiment a research company showed similar results for companies with respect to the number of the annual goals. What does this have to do with leadership? Leaders must arm themselves and must learn many things to help them mold their thoughts, words, and actions to have the most impact.

This research of number of goals/objectives versus results is paramount to a leader's ability to have an impact. The first of the four C's is competence. Competence is one of those concepts that people often misconstrue. Competence and wisdom (practical application of knowledge) are not passive. They are not something you simply possess because you spent time in an industry, role, or training but are revealed in how you act, how you apply what you learned or know, the results you realize, and how you react to the results.

I will now share the concept, context, and model I have found that help develop a person and organization in the 4 Cs. When it comes to character, compassion, and community I have found no better model than servant leadership. Servant Leadership is a theory introduced by Robert Greenleaf in 1977. Greenleaf was an executive, as well as a management researcher.

It Is said that he developed it through a combination of his research and his reading of Hermann Hesse's novella "Journey to the East." If you have not read it the story follows a group of men called the League who travel through time and space in search of the truth. It is a great read I suggest you find it.

To me one of the most important aspects of it is the realization that we humans are wired to not be able to see the truth without subjectivity. Based on this founding principle. Greenleaf theorized that a true leader must strive to create environments and circumstance to allow others to become what they are capable of... almost a mirror image of the Peter Principle where someone rises to the level of their own incompetence.

Luminous Leaders

Servant leadership strives for all people rising to their own competence as fed by developing their innate talents and capabilities. This is anathema to the often-narcissistic devotion of corporate managers from line to C-level to their own egos and to the Jack Welchian measure of corporate success: shareholder value above all else (and often to the exclusions of everything else).

As with most concepts or methodologies that become popular; many lazy opportunists simply learn the lingo and strew it about. Its as if they believe people will be fooled into thinking that they are truly champions of this new concept. They are often correct... temporarily at least. However, what they accomplish in the end is creating a distaste for the concept or theory on a wide scale.

It becomes a flavor of the day. Losing favor and slowly fading out of popularity. I've seen it happen with too many methods. It is sad. The irony being that the theory came to be seen because true adopters or champions were successful in a way that the rest wanted.

This success comes from true understanding. From implementing leveraging the context of this understanding and executing the most basic scientific approach most of us learned as children. Observe. Interpret. Form a hypothesis. Experiment. Learn. Adjust hypothesis. Lather. Rinse. Repeat, as necessary. Until you have turned the data (what you observed) into knowledge (your hypothesis) and created wisdom (continued verification of theory through practical application and observation of results) you have learned nothing.

At its most simple Servant Leadership is influencing the desired outcome (i.e. profit, culture, growth, success) by listening, understanding, and promoting others' ideas, talents, development, and actions. Not in a laissez faire anything goes kind of way. But from within an understanding of the direction the organization wants/ needs to go in and the realization it won't get there through dictatorship.

Flip the hierarchical pyramid upside down from a garbage runs downhill perspective without abandoning the responsibility of your management role. Once again management does not equal leadership. One can lead from anywhere in an organization. A good servant leader recognizes this and acts to cultivate, coach, and grow leaders whenever and wherever possible.

People are born with innate talents. Any talent can be developed to seed leadership. Leadership comes in many different flavors. A servant leader is like a master chef who takes the ingredients and tools available to them and creates the tastiest most fragrant concoction they can. Granted a tasty and fragrant concoction that people desire, want, and adopt. And, if possible, knows what additional flavors that will further enhance the present state, and then moves toward pulling these in from the outside or growing them within their own proverbial greenhouse.

"Great, so what do we DO with this?" This is an excellent question. But first let's address what the naysayers say about servant leadership as understood and as applied. Many an expert has developed models and such around Greenleaf's original speech and paper. My favorite is from the book "Seven

Pillars of Servant Leadership" (Sipe and Frick (2015)). There are seven pillars which demonstrate who servant leaders are:

1. Person of character

2. Puts people first

3. Skilled communicator

4. Compassionate collaborator

5. Has foresight

6. System thinker

7. Leads with moral authority

Some who proclaim to be servant leaders demonstrate some of these pillars but often fail in all. I believe that all of these are needed. A few can be leveraged from other people you are leading like system thinker and foresight but character, people first, communication, collaboration, and moral authority must be resident in said leader.

I would also argue that putting people first without the infrastructure of the other pillars and without competence is fraught with peril. The same can be said about any of the other pillars. What do these pillars mean? Character relates to integrity, humility, and morality. Within this context the leader can make decisions that are clear, authentic, and principled. Keep in mind that morality is not a religious construct but one of a sense of right or wrong within a code of ethics.

Putting people first to me relates to a coach/mentor mindset. What does any good coach/mentor do? They work hard to help develop others through a caring and collaborative relationship. Skilled communicator is not about how well someone can speak. It is more about how well they can listen.

Listening to determine what other's need, want, and feel as well as soliciting feedback. Feedback which they can truly assess and use to adjust attitudes, behaviors, and beliefs. It is only through this listening that they can communicate effectively and persuasively. This persuasion is not in a manipulative way but rather a leading for the greater and/or common good kind of way.

Compassionate collaborator is also based on listening and caring about the needs and concerns of others. It also is demonstrated by the ability to manage conflict, negotiate resolution, express appreciation, and build a highly skilled and integrated team environment. This attribute along with the other pillars allows for the leader to express appreciation and criticism in a manner which is most impactful to those on the receiving end.

This type of leader's message will rarely be thrown out with the bath water. Foresight is not about predicting the future but more about being able recognize opportunities and potential, create a clear vision, and taking as well as inciting bold actions to realize that future. This is done within a creative context in that many may not see the opportunities and potential and it is up to the leaders to provide. The leader creates the motivation, inspiration, and drive to help realize it.

Systems thinker around taking all parts and putting them within the context of how they are related. The ability to take complex and often convoluted environments and circumstance, see all the drivers and relationships, and plan a path forward in consideration of all of this.

As noted earlier, I believe that both foresight and systems thinking can be created through the combined knowledge and competency of the team. The people. Yes, the leader should take the reins and drive the group to understanding but for these two attributes it is a more of a collective than sole responsibility.

Finally, Leads with Moral Authority. Every group has its code of ethics. Quite often a group is challenged with the balance of ethics (doing the right things) with getting things done. The ethical or moral path is not always the easiest or quickest path. People look to the leader to guide them. Of all the seven pillars this is the one most people rely on to lead by example. I have been in too many organizations where there was a sort of "do as I say not as I do" attitude. To me, failing in this area strips one's stripes from their leader status.

Without accountability, of all team members there is none. Without moral authority there can be no respect, trust, or confidence. And without accountability, respect, trust, and confidence the pillars will crumble, and your team and your leadership will lie in ruins.

One of the worst managers I have ever had the experience of working for/with claimed to be a servant leader. She did so because the executives of our company promoted this style of management/leadership, and she was a corporate climber. I don't believe she ever studied or understood anything about servant leadership. I could provide examples where she violated the principles of every one of the seven pillars, but I will provide only one.

This company had the challenge of having to increase production by 5.5. times in six months. Some of the things that we needed to address was our attrition rate. For the factory floor we had a 90% attrition rate for the first six

months of employment. Combine that with the average time to go from new hire to "productive employee" was 1.5 years. "Productive employee" being measured as an employee skilled enough to perform all manufacturing steps on a single type of tool without help from others.

One other caveat was the competition for skilled mechanics was extremely high in our area. My team was given the task of addressing these three issues (reduce cycle time to increase throughput by 5.5 times, reduce attrition, and reduce cycle time from new to productive employee). I worked with our managing director to get the resources I needed from manufacturing, engineering, quality, and logistics. Of the ten team members only one was my direct report. Through the course of our project the self-proclaimed servant leader would come to our meetings, laugh at our ideas, and tell us what she thought we should do. We ignored her. After we implemented our solution, it met or exceeded all of its objectives (after some initial bumps). As such, it became the crown jewel of improvement at our site.

The main ideas and guidance came from me and the main design, implementation, and success was the result of the efforts of an employee in the "servant leader" organization. The site created a video celebrating our success and showing off the idea. In the video neither I nor the employee were acknowledged at all. The self-proclaimed servant leader who did things to disrupt us and nothing to help us was credited with the idea and one of her manager's who was not involved in the least was given credit for the implementation.

I ask you: which pillars of Servant Leadership did she uphold? NONE. Which did she crumble through her actions and attitudes? All the above. What's the lesson of this story? Beware of self-proclaimed anything. Judge a person by their attitudes, actions, and results. Bad things happen to good people, let the bad roll off like water off a duck's back.

Be your own person (don't allow others to bring or put you down) Don't be a poser. Work at learning, applying, and being the best you can be. Are Servant Leadership and the 4 Cs the only models of leadership worthy of your scrutiny? Absolutely not. They are just the two main models I use and practice to develop my style of leadership. I have decades of practice and results, and they have worked for me. I have provided them to give you context of where I am coming from.

The remainder of the chapter will be a broader stroke of my thoughts around leadership. I hope you see a tie between the thoughts, experiences, and ideas of Greenleaf, Drucker, Dorat, and Bentcover (that'd be me). Many people still believe true leaders are born not made. I hope you have realized that we are born with the type or style of leader we are to become but not all people ever become leaders. I believe we all have a leader within us and unfortunately too many of us buy into what others tell or "teach" us about ourselves.

They tell us we cannot do something, or we are or are not a certain way. We lead (pun intended) our lives through their lens without ever learning how to operate our own camera, exercise or develop our perspective.

Leadership is like potential energy. It lies within us until we choose to exercise it. If we never make the choice and/or take action it will never become kinetic. Until it becomes kinetic you will have no impact or influence on the world. The models and theories presented in this chapter provide a context within which anyone can develop or improve themselves as a leader. The choice is always yours.

Theories and models are starting points. Like the hypothesis in the scientific method, it is up to you to try them out, see results, assess the impact, and adjust, as necessary. Sometimes this will be completely abandoning a theory or model that does not work for you or more often simple adjustments again and again until you develop your own unique models, theories, and practices.

Move forward in a conscious and intentional way. Find who you are as a leader. Being conscious and intentional like this simply allows you to make a greater impact on the world around you (including your own). It will make it, so you make the world a better place and affect a better life for yourself and those around you. Be the leader only you can be.

Make the mark only you can make. We are waiting for you even if we don't know it. Even if you don't know it. Even if you are thinking I don't believe any of these things presented here… do you KNOW they are not true? Do you know they won't work for you? Do you not believe they worked for me? Even if you do, you may ask yourself so what? That's a great question. I don't pretend that just because these things worked for me, they will work for you.

I can tell you that all these things that worked for me, I learned from others. I may have tried them out and modified them to work better for me, but they started off as lessons from other's experience. Challenge your beliefs and attitudes. Try new things as you read about them or see them around you. Steel is forged through fire. So are leaders. Having said that, it is not effective to wait for a fire to figure out how to work through it. I have had several friends and read many books about people who are heroes. Or better said, people who performed heroic acts. Everyone of them stated they were nothing special; they were just able to act upon things they had learned in a conscious and intentional manner in an extreme circumstance.

The caveat there is they learned and practiced these things way before entering the "fire." No one becomes a leader by exercising their leadership to any affect in a sterile, static, or dead environment Also, no one leads when no one is around. They may act congruent with their thoughts and beliefs but have no impact until they interact with others.

Luminous Leaders

It is only through adversity, challenge, and change that a leader is born. Born through circumstances and action not simply from your mother's womb taking your first breath. It has been shown that DNA can pass things other than gender, hair color, eye color, skin tone, and our physicality but also certain instincts, attitudes, and behaviors. That later, can be leveraged and developed if you find the benefits.

If you make things conscious and intentional. You can only do this if you learn and/or develop models, make choices, and act within their construct. Even the smallest pebble can make a wave. It does not do so by laying on the ground. It does so by throwing itself in the water. The beauty of being human is we can choose to throw our pebble (ourselves) in the ocean.

As you approach the end of this chapter many of you may say or think that you have seen this all before. ALL these ideas are just academic. That is, they will not work in the REAL world. I once had a hiring manager tell me that my answer to his interview question was a "nice book answer." I was surprised. Realizing that was not a good attitude to have during an interview I took a breath, calmed down, and paused to think. I finally responded that the idea or model I used in the situation I relayed in my answer was framed from a textbook I had read and could have been a "nice book answer" had I simply practiced it as read, and it did not work in a real-world situation.

However, this real-world situation occurred many years after my initial read and I had (and still) taken the concept from the book, tried it out many times, put it in action, seen the results, and tweaked the textbook concept so it better fit, applied, and impacted the real-world circumstance I shared as I had done in many other instances.

As such, although the practice used was learned from a textbook, I have many examples of how and when I applied it in a real-life situation and my team realized positive results. Results which prove the theory as acted upon works.

I challenge you to take theses things and apply them. If they don't work cast them aside. Albeit not out of hand I would also challenge you to review the results and see if you could have modified your implementation of these in any way. If yes, alter them and try them again and keep doing so until you find what does work. If no, then cast them aside and find another theory or develop your own and try that out.

Isn't it worth a try? Too many of us are not willing to try anything new. We get stuck in a rut or habit and do the same thing repeatedly regardless of the results. There is a saying about if you do the same thing repeatedly expecting different results it is a sign of insanity. Being a believer in chaos theory I don't fully agree. But doing the same thing without assessing the results to me is insane. I am fascinated by how many people in work or in life simply do the same thing repeatedly without a care in the world about the results. It's as if the doing part is the important part. It is not. The impact and the results are not the only thing that matter but they matter a great deal.

Learn, act, assess, adjust, and achieve. Remember to celebrate your achievements just don't rest on them. If I had to make my own theory or model of leadership it would be founded on making your M.A.R.K. Model the behaviors, thoughts, attitudes, and beliefs you want to see in your organization, relationships, and the world. Be the example. That is the essence of leadership to me. Once again, the impact of those around you is the measure of leadership, not yourself alone.

Attack with authenticity. Do you what you say, say what you do, and admit when you're wrong.

Relate with reliability. Be consistent. Back up and support those around you. Nothing of importance gets done through the efforts of a single person. Review and practice the principles of Servant Leadership. Kill them with kindness. I've always had a love/hate relationship with that phrase but after years of practicing it (and not always succeeding) I like it. Be strong but coach, mentor, and support those around you to be their best. Don't waste time on those who will try to block you, shame you, or otherwise oppose you in some way. And they will ALWAYS be there. The best defense or counter to any negative thoughts, actions, or opinions is success. You are the author of your past, present, and future.

With respect to the blockers in your life don't be surprised if they immediately become your biggest "fan "when you succeed. And don't fret when they try (and often succeed) in taking partial or total credit for your success (i.e. the story of the self-proclaimed servant leader). This has happened to me too many times. It is a weird and annoying human phenomenon. I wish I could tell you I was always adept at not letting it go. The first time this happened I became so angry that I almost destroyed the success me and my team enjoyed. In the end I simply took a breath and relished in the joy of what me and my team accomplished for the organization. I also wish I could say that the former taking all the credit while doing nothing glory hounds all got their just desserts in the long run, but they did not.

I got over it finally when the CEO of a company I worked for gave a company speech. It was with a Fortune 50 company who had been losing market share to a European consortium for several years. Many of the company's employees cried about "unfair practices" (due to European laws which allowed the competitor to practice business in such a manner that they could undercut my company in price consistently). In his speech he told us to stop whining about "unfair practices." The laws which allowed our competitor to beat us on price were reality. No amount of whining was going to change European or U.S. laws. We need to focus on the quality of our work and product. We needed to beat our European competitors on value not price.

It took a few years of consistent vision and practice, but this company eventually got its market share back. That CEO was a true leader. He listened to people. He assessed the situation. He communicated clearly about the results, our reality, and provided a path forward. Not only that but he was consistent in his work and action. He truly made his M.A.R.K.

As you may see with my and stories about leadership, it is not all rainbows and unicorns. In my experience it almost NEVER is. The juice for me is seeing people develop and thrive as well as getting results that have a positive impact on my relationships, organizations, clients, and companies I relate with. If you have made it to the end of this chapter I thank you for reading.

My style of writing, leadership, and thought is not for everyone. And that is one of the main points I want you to take away. Don't adopt someone else's style in ANYTHING. Find your own. A mentor of mine used to tell me: leaders are readers. With most adages this is an oversimplification which we can use to remind us of a concept. Leaders are a certain kind of reader. A reader of words, people, the situation.

As you grow as a leader your intuition will grow as well. Develop with intention and purpose and then learn to trust it. I hope these words connected with you and helps you on your journey to become the best leader you can be. If not, the beauty of a book like this is that every chapter is from a different perspective. A different voice.

Find the few or one that resonates with you. Remember we all have similarities, but we are all also unique. The similarities help us connect and our uniqueness (when found, embraced, and nourished) helps propel us forward. Go lead. Impact the world in a positive way. Live and lead a rich and fulfilled life.

Mark.bentcover@gmail.com

~ MichaelNoble Emeghara ~

Dr. Noble is known as TheMindGuru and is an Author, Peace Ambassador, Poet, Humanitarian, International Celebrity Author, and Guinness World Records Author and is the History First Mental Interviewer. He is the distinguished 3x Celebrity Award Winning International Speaker, the International Ambassador of Peace, The Global Humanitarian Icon and was the African Representative in The Global Pandemic Summit. He is the First Person in African History to Win 3 International Awards Through Public Speaking on the same day and time and is a Guinness World Records Author and 3x World Records Humanitarian. He is known as one of the global tops in mentally 100 greatest minds in history and was branded The Mind Guru of The World by The World's Most Influential Author the Celebrity Guru Dr Pravin Patel. Pravin was also coached by the greatest speakers of all time in 2020 with his learning partners Success Resources, Real Success Resources, Raymond Aaron Mastery of Greatness, Think and Grow Rich Screening during the pandemic and in 2021 post pandemic.

Testimonials

The Greatest Mind Guru of All Time by United Nations Peace Ambassador Dr Pravin Patel (Mentor)

The King of Encouragement and Support by Think and Grow Rich Ambassador (Mentor) Sarah Lee Mba.

A kind of wonderful person (Think and Grow Rich Foundation Founder Don Green)

A very kind-hearted person (World's #1 Motivational Speaker Daughter, Serena Brown Travis.

Top 100 of the Mentally Greatest in History

(Guinness World Records International Celebrity Author and Speaker Nadene Joy)

RECOGNITIONS

He is most grateful to be recognized by Oprah Winfrey , Oprah Winfrey Network (OWN)Aware Magazine, Forbes Magazine, Time Magazine, The Rolling Stone, Sharon Lecther, Sara Blakeley, Sirbalo Comedy, Les Brown, Eric Thomas, Jay Shetty, Robin Sharma, Robert Kiyosaki, Kevin Trudeau, Sarah Lee Mba, Joel Diamonds, Nelson Mandela, Dr Pravin Patel, Greg Hana, Bob Proctor, Raymond Aaron, Robert J Moore, Amanda M Renaud, Serena Brown Travis, Forbes Business Council, Noble World Records, Fearless motivation, Fearless soul, Bindu Badu and others. It is with deep Joy in my heart I co authored my first book with Robert J Moore, Pravin Patel, Serena Brown Travis,

Raymond Aaron and other authors across the globe. I am humbled to share the international celebrity virtual stage with The UN Peace Ambassador to Canada Dr Pravin Patel, The King of Inspiration in The World Amb Powerful Steve, The world's #1 digital citizen Main Steel, Global Business Leaders like Dr Daphne Soares, Rosalyn Kahn and #1 Success mentor Raymond Aaron alongside Swami Vishwa Amanda the mother of The World.

He is a History First Mental Interviewer after mentally interviewing 100+ of the greatest Speakers and got Coached, recognized, became friends, and shared the virtual stages, join the same group with them through observation and mimicking their success system on Facebook.

Michael is also the 3x International Best-selling Author, Nominated In 5 Different Categories as A Bestseller In my First Book Magnetic Entrepreneur World Renowned. A book endorsed by the former American President Donald Trump.

Michaelnoble is also the Co- author and Bestselling author in 8 different categories in Don't Judge a Book by Its Cover (Rich hearts can be in poor clothe) and Guinness World Records Book Go Getters: Getting It Done.

I am a Magnetic Entrepreneur Inc VIP and Affiliated with Magnetic Entrepreneur Inc Canada. A Member in The Hollywood EzWay Wall of Fame USA and Global Nominee EzWay Wall of Fame Awards 2021. He is in partnership with many international organisations and in a lifetime partnership with the United Nations Peace Ambassador to Canada equally an official member in the Global Genius Generation Group More especially he is a lifelong learner.

Luminous Leaders

His Highness Hon Royal Amb Dr Michael is also an Ancestral Royal Ambassador Under Supreme Council of African Royalties and Kings in Ikemba 1 Of Africa Royal Family Ulakwo Etche. The World Peace Ambassador to Canada and World Peace Ambassador to United Kingdom both under Her Royal Majesty Queen of Africa Queen Uba Iwunwa. His Royal Highness is the Certified royal citizen of the worldwide empire of David Isreal and Royal Ambassador of South Africa Bakhoidan San Kingdom Of South Africa under His Majesty Prof Dr Jeremy Saffier.

Miraculously, he did all these things above inside his humble room in a little community in Imerienwe Ngor Okpala Imo state Nigeria during the pandemic and post pandemic.

He is the recipient of twenty-one Honorary doctorate degree in peace and humanities and 200+ International Awards for my service to humanity in Africa, Asia, South America, North America, and Europe. which includes Global Humanitarian Icon Awards (Global Deep Daan Foundation) International Ambassador of Peace, Nobel Peace Prize Award and Leader of World Peace 2021 by Prof Abdullghani Yahya Al-ebarh, Nobel Environmental Prize 2021, International Golden Environment Art Award,17 Doctorate in Humanities, Peace, Environment from Right to Save Life Foundation, Nobel Peace Prize Awardee by Prof Abdullghani, Egypt (Sovereign Kingdom of Atlantis) etc. International Women Day Declarators Award, Speaker at

The World Spiritual Celebration, Fathers Day Celebration, African Representative at The Global Pandemic Summit, International Celebrity Award, Global Peace Ambassador Iqra Foundation, Leadership Award from Agaram foundation, Peace Builder Award, Peace Champion, Living Legend Award from Pheonix Book of World Records Leadership Rights to save life, World Peace Tree Advocate, Winning Author at

International Celebrity Author Awards Canada. In additional to all the above, he is an Executive Contributor at World's #1 Inspirational Magazine Brainz and equally A Global Advisor of Hope at Global Movement of Hope Canada owned by his Co Author World Renowned Nadene Joy.

Michaelnoble received six Global Oscars for Global Professionals 2022 in Philippines the Most Outstanding Influential Celebrity Author of All time and The Most Inspiring Man on Earth Award in Delhi India Golden book Of the Earth to name but a few. His Mission, vision and purpose is to use practical proven techniques to awaken, motivate and inspire seven billion people through his story using the self-help Industry, media houses, movies, magazines to let them know that it can be done and have any and everything the desire in life if the are willing to change their mindsets and their mindset paradigms.

~ Chapter 7 ~

Dr. MichaelNoble Emeghara

~ The Power of Decisions in Leadership ~

What is Leadership? Have you asked yourself this simple but interesting question. To lead is to become a good follower and for one become a good follower that person must become a good listener. Everything falls on leadership in the other hands you cannot lead if you cannot listen. Leadership is the act of listening to an authority and doing exactly what you are being told to do. Everyone is a leader. First a leader of yourself, then your family.

An individual lives grows or disintegrates because of Leadership. Leadership requires sacrifice, love to crown it all for without there will never be unity among leaders in business.

An individual controls their lives by asking good questions and listening to get answers. Sometimes the reverse is the case like my encounter with the lecturer in the University of Nigeria Nsukka 2017 when I was humiliated because I wanted to know the truth about the present economy but was humiliated and called stupid, crazy, and mad.

My decision to go extra miles on what school wasn't instructing the students. I left the classroom to my village to find the answers to my question.

Luminous Leaders

There are only two sources of genuine information that's science and religion well I went to God in 3 days fasting and prayers without water. On the 7th of August 2017 God sent his Angel in my dream who came with the message The Mind Arena Faith Speaks Life. I have dedicated my entire life to make sure that this message which was an idea became an Academy which have reached thousands of people international.

Leadership is all about decision making and sticking to it. My decision led me to God and He showed me life plan which have given me the opportunity to be part of Guinness World Records and other world records Co author books, become a peace ambassador etc. When an individual decides to change their lives and have a strong will with a great determination the universe will conspire and make that dream become a reality.

I will end with my eternal quote which says "the illiterates of our society will not be those that didn't go to School rather those that failed to use the mind technology given to mankind by the maker" truly an abundant mind brings with it an abundant life.

Connect with me using the following links.

YouTube
https://youtube.com/@Themindarenaacademy?si=S6283Qn OUE1w2JOQ

TikTok

https://vm.tiktok.com/ZM6b5tMx1/

Instagram
https://www.instagram.com/michaelnobleemeghara?igsh=YzljYTk1 ODg3Zg==

Luminous Leaders

Facebook

https://www.facebook.com/michaelnoble.emeghara?mibextid=ZbWKwL

LinkedIn

https://www.linkedin.com/in/michaelnoble-emeghara-a314121a9?utm_

Twitter X

https://x.com/DEmeghara44197/status/1737291628564427143?s=20

Email us for your Conferences and build your confidence with our 6 years experience by emailing us @

emegharamichaelnoble@gmail.com

~ Conclusion ~

Amanda M Renaud

Leadership needs are forever changing based on goals and needs of a team. Leadership dynamics will change and sometimes for the best. With a willingness, drive to build together and the ability to recognise difference as strength. Difference can be viewed as strength rather than a hindrance, and that a is powerful approach. There are no limitations on what can be achieved with this level of recognition. Leadership can be a very difficult journey but its one of the most rewarding positions to be in. To be able to serve others and begin to build something together that serves purpose is a wonderful accomplishment and all milestones of leadership should be celebrated.

Being a leader who celebrates others and teaches rather than disciplines, is something that I feel is a critical approach overall to leadership. Being a leader who models the behaviors and attitudes is also such an important factor to consider when leading. Every leader will make mistakes that are inevitable, but it comes down to transparency, authenticity, and accountability.

A leader who owns their mistakes and makes a continual effort to grow and learn is a luminous leader that has something to share. All leaders have different styles and strategies, and less seasoned leaders often struggle in the beginning without adequate support.

Luminous Leaders

Being a leader requires different strategies for different individuals. What worked for one, will not always work for everyone. Leadership requires a profound awareness and creative deployment of strategies to get through to your team.

I have found that despite the information available today and we have more now than ever, people still lack communication skills which in turn acts as a barrier to progression. Excellent communication is mandatory when pursuing leadership roles and working with others. Leadership is not just about getting daily tasks done, its about creating other luminous leaders who empower, teach, and support the environments around them.

A trusted leader who communicates effectively and offers safety, support and compassion will always outperform talent. These luminous leaders often create top tier leaders who making lasting impressions on their team and organizations. Luminous Leadership is worth sharing and working towards, you never know who is watching and seeking the skills you have to offer. There will be good days and days of defeat when it comes to leadership and the beauty of it is that you either win or you learn.

Leadership is not about fancy titles or the organization to do list. Many leaders struggle to balance operational tasks and leading their team. Often most organizations have gaps and areas where improvement or change needs to occur and someone who can identify these areas and slowly work on them, will be noticed and progress can be made.

Leaders who are self-aware and dedicated to serving with humility are needed and we have seen how poor leadership can quickly sink a ship. When a leader leads with no agenda and merely from a place of compassion, there is no limit to what can be achieved. Of course, everyone plays an important role but modeling these behaviors and inspiring others to try their best, is a leader who will never be forgotten and will sow their seeds of hope within others.

We have seen enormous shifts in leadership and expectations in recent years, there is a huge demand for good leaders who celebrate diversity and find ways to fill the voids and empty that exist within the places and faces we often lead. A leader must always consider that others can not give you what they do not have having an awareness of others needs, areas of improvement, their goals and the organizations goals is important to understand in depth and be analyzing. Unmet needs can cause very tense and toxic environments. A leader who has this understanding can quickly curb conflict and high turn over when they understand the people and environment around them.

A leader who makes the people they serve their primary focus is often trusted and highly respected. Good rapport and healthy relationships are key to building successful teams. An ignored problem is a growing problem. Leaders who ignore the needs, goals and accomplishments of their team often end up creating more harm than they often foresee. Ignoring the needs of others and their concerns often leads to toxic work environments, imposter syndrome and burn out. It perpetuates cycles that affect everyone. Many experience high-stress and burn out and the cost involved in turning these issues around can be quite expensive. Not just cost wise either, word of mouth is powerful or being viewed as a negative leader can be quite terrible with many consequences.

People will always remember how you treated them and made them feel inside. Whether the concerns are small or large in nature is irrelevant, it matters that they are acknowledged and dealt with before they grow into something that hinders success. Everything is important and valuable; behavior is a language and as a leader understanding that is critical. If you see someone struggling as a leader, exploring it can derail a ton of other potential problems.

Leaders can get caught up in taking things personal or making it personal. A luminous leader doesn't need to react or focus on the behavior in depth, but they ensure they have all the details, the "whys," and causations. Luminous Leaders understand that "people are not giving them a hard time but rather having a hard time. The leader who is brave enough to have the hard conversations and make the people they serve around them a priority are the leaders who make huge contributions and impact. Being a leader who listens to understand rather than punish is a leader who has a grasp on serving others. Understanding and focusing on solutions as well as precautionary measures that protect the people and organization have a strong foundation that will be successful in their endeavours. Any business IS the business of people. Luminous Leaders must embrace this aspect as important. Being able to communicate, serve and work with others is one of the main foundational elements.

It takes a level of commitment and growth to be an effective leader who shares, teaches, and empowers. Leadership is a lifelong process. The people you serve, and the causes will require you to have a sense of resilience because there will always be tough days and days that make the journey worth it. Many leaders often lose themselves through the struggle and hardships of everyday life and so being someone who offers something different that captures the essence of what it is to shine while lifting others up is Luminious and a rare commodity in today's corporate world.

The people who really want the chance to be leaders and help improve the environment around them are rare. Most people today are consumed with their own lives and responsibilities. Someone who wants to try and is not focused on their own personal gain but the gain of the organization, is extremely rare. Somone who cares about your business or organization as much as you do is someone who will do a great job if they have the support or tools needed to be successful.

Many people will often be distracted and go through a period of questioning when things are not going so well and its so helpful for others when we offer them support and really hear their concerns. Being a leader who shows up no matter what and is transparent can move the people around them to do wonderful things. A leader who sees their team as valuable, competent, and capable is a leader who builds strong foundational roots. When the roots are rotten the plant cannot thrive, teams work is the same way. Strong roots and foundations are the key to building lasting teams. Every member involved has a role to play and what they offer and contribute is important. When we as leaders see others with positive attitudes and focus on their growth too, they will see it as important. If you want others to care, you also must care. Life is a mirror and what you present will always be looking back at you.

Balance and application are what makes a luminous leader really shine. Goals without any action or application simply will not work. Application and action are much needed elements to leadership and success.

Luminous Leaders

www.ingramcontent.com/pod-product-compliance
Lightning Source LLC
Chambersburg PA
CBHW052326220526
45472CB00001B/287